BÔ YIN RÂ
(JOSEPH ANTON SCHNEIDERFRANKEN)

VOLUME TWO
OF THE 32-VOLUME CYCLE
THE GATED GARDEN

THE BOOK ON
THE LIVING GOD

SECOND EDITION

For more information
about the books of Bô Yin Râ and
titles available in English translation,
visit the Kober Press web site at
www.kober.com

THE KOBER PRESS PUBLISHES THE ONLY ENGLISH TRANSLATIONS
OF THE BOOKS OF BÔ YIN RÂ AUTHORIZED BY THE KOBER VERLAG,
SWITZERLAND. THE KOBER VERLAG PUBLISHES THE BOOKS OF BÔ YIN RÂ
IN THE ORIGINAL GERMAN AND HAS PROTECTED THEIR INTEGRITY
SINCE THE AUTHORS'S LIFETIME.

BÔ YIN RÂ
(JOSEPH ANTON SCHNEIDERFRANKEN)

THE BOOK ON THE LIVING GOD

TRANSLATED FROM THE GERMAN
BY B.A. REICHENBACH

THE KOBER PRESS

BERKELEY, CALIFORNIA

First edition English translation ©1991
by B. A. Reichenbach

Second edition English translation ©2014
by B. A. Reichenbach

Eric W. Strauss, Publisher

Eric W. Strauss & Malka Weitman, Editors

All rights reserved

For permission to quote or excerpt, contact The Kober Press
Email: koberpress@mindspring.com

This book is a translation from the German of *Das Buch vom lebendigen Gott*, Basel-Leipzig: Kober'sche Verlagsbuchhandlung, 1927. The copyright to the German original is held by Kober Verlag AG, Bern, Switzerland.

Printed in the United States of America

International Standard Book Number: 978-0-915034-25-3

Page design, typography and composition by Dickie Magidoff

Cover design by John Watson

CONTENTS

Word of Guidance 7
1 "The Tabernacle of God is with Men" 15
2 The White Lodge 29
3 Meta-Physical Experiences 39
4 The Inner Journey 57
5 The En-Sof 95
6 On Seeking God 105
7 On Leading an Active Life 111
8 On "Holy Men" and "Sinners" 117
9 The Hidden Side of Nature 125
10 The Secret Temple 139
11 Karma 147
12 War and Peace 161

13	The Unity among Religions	173
14	The Will to Find Eternal Light	183
15	The Human Being's Higher Faculties of Knowing	191
16	On Death	203
17	On the Spirit's Radiant Substance	215
18	The Path toward Perfection	229
19	On Everlasting Life	245
20	The Spirit's Light Dwells in the East	255
21	Faith, Talismans, and Images of God	269
22	The Inner Force in Words	281
23	A Call from Himavat	291
	Giving Thanks	299
	Epilogue	305
	Reminder	311
	Editor's Note to the Second Edition	313

WORD OF GUIDANCE

You should not read this book if you believe the teachings of your faith with heart and soul.

You should not read this book if you have never doubted God.

❧

This book is written for all those who suffered bitter conflicts in themselves in their unceasing quest, but who, for all their labors, never found God's Being.

It is addressed to all who are tormented by thorns of gnawing doubt.

Such readers will find help in it.

For them this book will mark the way.

❧

The Book on the Living God

What I shall here convey is wisdom rooted in the ages.

The few in every generation who had the faculty of comprehending it have kept that knowledge secret since the dawn of time.

Only on a few, exceptional occasions was it possible in earlier days to tell the world of this most ancient wisdom, and even then it had to be disguised in dark, symbolic language.

But now the time has come to speak of it more plainly, given that distorted fragments of this knowledge have been, and continue to be, spread throughout the world by minds who have no calling to disclose it.

And so it was decided, in the Spirit's inner East, to open for the nations of the West the sacred shrine that had so long been carefully protected from the gaze of the profane.

That shrine is here unlocked by one who has been authorized.

❧

But anyone who seeks to enter must yet be tried and strictly tested; and none shall ever cross the threshold of the Temple who has not proven worthy.

Word of Guidance

Thus, I here can show the reader only from afar what those who proved themselves shall one day come to understand.

What words are able to convey about the Temple's mysteries, I shall not fail to tell you.

If you would search their very depth, however, you must endeavor to experience them within your inmost self.

These mysteries shall not reveal themselves, except to those who strive to comprehend them with all their energies and strength.

By merely "reading" what I here present you shall be gaining very little.

What is transmitted here in words must meet with willing hearts—hearts that shall receive and guard it in themselves—for else it has been given voice in vain.

However, none can form a valid judgment as to the merits—or defects—of what is being stated in this book, but those who passed the stringent tests that all must undergo who seek to be admitted to the Temple.

Only those who know this Temple from within can form objective judgments.

AND SO I HERE can show you only from without what shall one day reveal itself within the inmost self of readers who have understood what I convey.

In order that it may reveal itself you need a resolute, untiring will to reach your highest goal; and only those found strong enough to force such will to serve them can hope to see my words confirmed within their own experience.

They, indeed, will find the way that leads them to their Living God.

And in themselves they shall discover the kingdom of the Spirit and its eternal hierarchies.

Their Living God shall then be born in their eternal self.

❧

I DO NOT SEEK to offer "proof" for what I have to say.

Whether my disclosures state the truth you must determine for yourself.

For only in yourself abides the silent judge who shall confirm what you may feel as you absorb my words.

Word of Guidance

The "proofs" I have to offer would tell you very little; for none of you has gone the arduous ways that I once had to travel.

Moreover, in the Spirit's realm there are no proofs of "universal" cogency.

Here, all will find the only proof convincing them within their own eternal self.

༄

WHAT I PRESENT is not a scientific discipline, nor is it a religious creed.

I merely show you all that can be shown of the eternal wisdom of the Spirit's inner East: the mystery surrounding the radiant Temple of Eternity.

May my words encourage you to wake up and regain your timeless self at last; for to this day you still are not yet conscious of the self you truly are.

May inner strength and blessings be with all who manifest good will and firm resolve!

༄

CHAPTER ONE

"THE TABERNACLE OF GOD IS WITH MEN"

REVELATION 21:3

LONG AGO THE WESTERN WORLD HAD quietly received a message of enlightened knowledge from the East, and thus it learned, in images reflecting Christian faith, about a wondrous Brotherhood of spiritual guides and helpers present here on earth. The nations of the West did not, however, comprehend the revelation that had reached them in this form.

Thus, legends came to grow and spun their web around the Holy Grail and its majestic knighthood.

Knowledge offering profoundest solace was lost in a perplexing myth, and so became the fabled background for much faith-inspired poetry.

BUT NOW, IN our day, there suddenly appeared exotically embellished stories, spread by enterprising mystagogues who openly told all the world about initiated "adepts" and "mahatmas" —wise men living in seclusion in the heart of Asia—who were endowed with secret knowledge. These tales betrayed at once, however, albeit unintentionally, that their inventors, while having learned about those hidden sages, had never seen one face-to-face; for else they could not have imagined that various performing fakirs and other curious "holy men" whom they had met might actually be members of that spiritual Brotherhood.

But since in the subconscious life of many souls there still survives a last faint sense of human mortals being in some way connected with a sanctuary of God's Spirit—a Temple hidden somewhere on this earth—there soon emerged a circle of believers who felt they might establish contact with that hidden shrine.

Regrettably, they set out on mistaken paths and to this day continue searching in the wrong direction.

From bits and pieces of old knowledge lying on the way they put together a novel "scientific"

"The Tabernacle of God is with Men"

system of "spiritual" instruction and research, based upon a "secret doctrine"; for in their innocence they honestly believed that conscious knowledge of the Spirit—which comprehends eternity—could in effect be learned the way that one acquires knowledge of the mind.

They practice strict asceticism, to make themselves, as they believe, more "spiritual"; they steep themselves in the miasmas of a mysticism rising from the fever-ridden jungles of the East; they scour every nook and cranny searching for instructions, old or new, on how one masters occult powers—and by such means assume that one might find those hidden guides, who look on all such doings with only pity and amusement.

Among so many seekers none will scale the rock-hewn path ascending to the sunlit peaks of the Great Mountains; instead, all trudge along the wide and dusty roads through stifling valleys to worship at some long since desecrated shrine.

※

Many thought they were already on the way that leads one to the clear-eyed sovereigns who rule within the Spirit's realm, and now they roam the forests, searching for a "holy man."

Others are of the opinion that the hidden wisdom of those unknown sages is nothing more than the tradition of religious teachings of the East.

And so they reason, quite correctly, saying:

"In former days we, too, had our prophets and enlightened seers; we, too, have sacred writings from most ancient times.

"God's reality, however, is everywhere the same.

"Why, then, should we, whose heritage is of the West, now seek our soul's salvation only in the East?"

Their reasoning is valid; for if it merely were a question of finding that which any pious human soul on earth can learn to realize within itself and on its own; or if one only had in mind the ancient teachings that still govern the religious concepts of the East, then all, indeed, could reach fulfillment by themselves and in the wise instructions they received from prophets and great teachers of their people.

⚘

YET NEITHER the wisdom, nor the quiet work of those who rule within the Spirit has much in common with the teachings of Eastern religions; for the Spirit's secret helpers are guiding human

"The Tabernacle of God is with Men"

souls beyond the kind of heaven that every age created, by virtue of its faith, as an expression of its deepest yearnings.

The guardians of all humanity's primordial heritage are the most powerful protectors of every human's spiritual nature. At the same time, in this earthly life, they are the human being's truest and most understanding friends and helpers.

Since ages immemorial they have been sending Brothers from their midst to all parts of the earth, who then created focal points of spiritual energy wherever there was need.

Through the ages they have found their spiritual Sons and Brothers among all nations of the earth. The Spirit's law itself, however, will determine whom they choose.

But those who have been chosen all recognize a site in central Asia as their spiritual birthplace on this planet. It is a site where no one finds admittance who has not been invited.

The few that since the dawn of time resided here together never enter life on earth in mortal form.

This task they will assign, instead, to those among their spiritual Sons and Brothers who were chosen by eternal law to take an active part in physical existence.

They themselves are but the guardians who faithfully protect a treasure in the kingdom of the Spirit that mortal human beings once possessed—before their Fall into the realm of matter.

They generate the spiritual energy which those of their elected Brothers who are active in the world require, if they are to perform their labors in the service of all humankind.

Would it not be simple-minded to assume that these sublime immortals might ever be Buddhists, Brahmans, lamas, pundits, let alone performing fakirs?

Nor should one take those guardians to be all-knowing experts in the pseudo-science that would study the occult.

All such ideas are fundamentally in error.

༄

THE LUMINARIES, who mediate eternal Light, are first and foremost active agents here on earth.

Their Elders, the immortal Fathers, have never known the human mortal's "thirst for knowledge," nor could they even have experienced this desire.

The Luminaries, on the other hand, who are at once their spiritual Sons and Brothers, have long ago outgrown the mortal mind's insatiable curiosity.

None of them is interested in converting humankind to the teachings of Eastern mysticism and philosophy.

To them it matters little whether you believe in the Bible, the Koran, the Vedas, or in the teachings of the Buddha.

Among the followers of all these faiths, however, they always find some individuals to whom they can send help and guidance, even if the souls they counsel and protect are often unaware of how this inner contact comes about.

The Luminaries, who convey eternal Light, do not intend to give you doctrines that you must believe; instead, they want to build for you the inner bridge connecting you—the creature-fettered mortal of this world—with the eternal kingdom of the Spirit and its radiant substance.

But they reject all practices that seek to lash a person's consciousness into a state of ecstasy, in which the human mind—no longer master of its senses—may then hallucinate about its power of making God descend upon itself.

They clearly also know that one cannot attain through intellectual exertion that which antecedes all human thought and whose reality lies far beyond the grasp of mental comprehension.

They only smile when seeing those who look upon themselves as gods in mortal guise.

But they shall offer help and guidance, without being seen, to all who strive to find their Living God within.

They are the true and real high priests of the Spirit whose cup of blessings will give strength to every pilgrim seeking God with heart and soul.

※

Surely, you will recognize the difference between those spiritual helpers and the alleged "adepts" of occult research who function in that stew of shrouded mystical traditions, gathered from all corners of the earth, which its creators named "Theosophy"—the wisdom of God.

This kind of "theosophy," pursued by self-deluded dreamers, with its required exercises, meditations and fasting, will not—for all your purity in

"The Tabernacle of God is with Men"

thought and deed, for all your knowledge touching things one need not know—advance you by a single step toward that sublimest goal you long to reach and whose existence you may sense within your heart.

You well may end up as a fool; if not, indeed, become what you and others call a "saint"; but never shall you in this manner find your God.

※

IF WHAT YOU seek is nothing more than what you can at all times find within you, independent of the Spirit's help, then you clearly need not fix your eyes upon the inner East.

The guides whose help you are receiving from that hidden realm—even if they lived in your own city or, for that matter, your own house—have other things to give you.

They can create within you what you never could bring forth yourself. A force that shall take root in you and for whose life your being shall prove sustenance.

A force you do not now possess, nor ever could attain out of your self alone.

Indeed, not even Luminaries, who mediate eternal light, are able to attain it on their own.

They only would restore to you what you had once possessed: before desire to experience life within this world of matter caused you of necessity to lose it.

The Elders of the spiritual Brotherhood have never been without it, because they did not know the Fall into the realm of matter, into the body of a mortal creature here on earth.

Never having tasted death, they are alive on earth today—as they have been through the millennia—in bodies formed of purest spiritual substance, which does not perish, nor decay.

They were never born into a mortal creature organism, such as you and I.

However, in the Spirit's world they raised, as their elected Brothers, certain human spirits that had once endured the Fall and, thus, were due to be embodied in a mortal organism: in order that these Brothers, once incarnate here on earth, might then accomplish tasks which in this world can only be accomplished by virtue of a mortal body.

And in this way they even now prepare their future Brothers for a coming age.

Their true location on this earth, however: the site from which their help proceeds, has been since ancient times—when first the human animal became a vessel to receive the human spirit's timeless self—a center, near the highest mountains on this planet, which no one can approach whose spirit they will not themselves invite into their midst.

※

HERE, INDEED, the "Tabernacle of God" is found on earth "with men."

Here, with energies of purest spiritual substance, the kingdom of the Spirit reaches down into this planet's physical events.

From here, eternal Light goes forth in rays of purest spiritual substance, reaching all who dwell on earth.

But far too many people on this earth still seek the Spirit's light in vain, because their searches lead them in the wrong direction.

To all of them I here can only offer the advice that they should turn around; because the living light proceeding from the inner East will not be able to infuse them while their eyes continue to be blinded by the many lights that humans kindled through the ages: all the lamps and torches they had lit, attempting in their fallen state—embodied in a mortal creature body—to penetrate the darkness on their path.

Only those, indeed, whose eyes are not distracted by the constant glitter of this world, but who, instead, keep calmly looking toward the inner East, will there discover living light on holy mountains.

Once having found it, that light will shine upon their way until they shall have reached their goal—until they shall have reached their goal.

CHAPTER TWO

THE WHITE LODGE

In the vocabulary of theosophy the title "Great White Brotherhood" is meant to signify the spiritual helpers of humanity on earth, and as this term is now in use, it is retained here for that purpose. Still, it should be noted that the members of that body merely recognize that term, but do not use it as a name among themselves.

Their strict seclusion from the outside world may seem to justify that one conferred upon that purely spiritual body a name suggesting some connection with Freemasonry; namely, the "White Lodge," a title given them in German. As a body, this spiritual Brotherhood is without equal among associations on this planet. There are no forms of human fellowship to which this Brotherhood might be compared, not even in a figurative sense.

The members of that body never meet in person, except when circumstances make it unavoidable, and seldom do they write each other letters.

Yet, on the spiritual plane, they live in permanent, uninterrupted contact and community of knowledge; forming, in effect, a single consciousness in the dimension of the soul.

This Brotherhood was not established by external laws or rules.

All of its members share complete equality, but each one knows the place assigned to him alone, which is determined by his given spiritual endowment and potential.

They all, however, of their own free will obey the same supreme authority, in whom they recognize their spiritual head.

That head is not elected nor appointed, but none belonging to this Brotherhood will ever be in doubt concerning his identity.

ೞ

MEMBERSHIP IN this eternal body is not obtained by formal application, nor can one gain it by deceptive means or force.

The White Lodge

Whether someone is to be admitted depends alone on certain undiscoverable laws within the Spirit, which will affect a person's innate faculties. But where this is the case, no might on earth could ever hinder his admission.

Those having been admitted are not, however, bound by any promise, pledge, or vow.

They are themselves their only law and norm.

One cannot recognize the members of that body by any outward sign, nor by some shared characteristics in their way of life.

They, on the other hand, will know a member of their circle, even if they never met before, whenever need arises that they meet in person; and they will recognize each other without password, sign, or grip.

⁂

Owing to its very nature, this Brotherhood's identity must needs be hidden from the outside world; yet many individuals, indeed whole nations have at times been guided by its spiritual influence.

No mortal ever entered any path toward higher, nonmaterial goals without the unseen help and guidance of a member of that Brotherhood, or of that body as a whole.

Those who are receiving spiritual guidance very seldom know of or suspect the unseen influence to which they owe their very best.

But in cases showing more developed spiritual awareness, this influence of inner help is felt indeed; only it is then attributed, almost without exception—owing either to deficient insight, or misled by superstitious concepts—to powers of the "super-natural."

༄

To be sure, the realm of fantasy, where writers of all times and regions found poetic inspiration, owes to this misunderstanding a wealth of its colorful characters.

Fantasy has ever been the poets' friend; for pure and simple truth is far too unaffected and austere to let herself be draped in the luxurious garments of a poet's fancy.

Wrong interpretation of the spiritual help provided by the silent circle of humankind's elder Brothers here on earth has equally enriched the myths and legends of religion.

The White Lodge

From time to time, however, there have been individuals who consciously perceived the influence and presence of that invisible, eternal body, which nonetheless reveals itself through living human mortals. But others then obscured again, with doubts of every kind, all traces pointing to such knowledge, so that at last mere enigmatic tales remained, which still suggested here and there that more was known about these things in earlier days; indeed, that certain human souls must have experienced insights of profound significance in this connection.

But then, in our time, some overly enthusiastic minds had come to know of the existence of that spiritual body. Only the simplicity of all its spiritual work and nature did so little satisfy the colorful imagination of these visionaries that they found it necessary to embellish their accounts about the Brotherhood with some exotic touches. Thus, humankind's elder—namely, spiritually older—Brothers were dressed up more like demigods, at least as mighty sorcerers, who, of course, had long since known whatever modern science is only now beginning to explore and who were, in addition, generously furnished with all the magical resources ever dreamed up by oriental fabulists.

It would appear those seekers erred here in good faith, trusting that the end would surely justify the means if they endeavored to enthrone the inaccessible immortals, of whom they had some vague idea, high above all humankind. In this they saw themselves confirmed by some quite vulgar fakir tricks, which were naively taken as conclusive proof that their performers were authentic members of that "Great White Brotherhood."

Those, however, to whom this name supposedly refers: the spiritual Luminaries who mediate eternal Light—the priesthood serving in the Temple of Eternity on earth—thoroughly reject all idle masquerades.

They know full well that they are human beings, quite like other mortals on this earth; except that, owing to their higher spiritual age, they can assume their given place within the Spirit's hierarchy and, thus, are able to convey to all their fellow mortals, energies of spiritual substance. However, they do not themselves create the energies that they transmit.

༄

To be sure, the Brotherhood in its reality presents a far more dignified and worthy sight than even the most colorful imagination might envisage.

The silent influence exerted by the members of that body encompasses all fields of humanity's spiritual development.

The threads their hands are guiding will sometimes lead to works revealing highest human creativity; at other times they end in centers of great worldly power.

They, indeed, are able to move mountains without lifting even a finger, because their timeless will—purely guided by the Spirit's light and purged of every personal desire—is the effective force behind the will of not a few who then cause other hands and minds to be employed and active.

For occult powers of the sort that fakirs seek to master there truly is no place in the activities of human beings' elder Brothers.

Their task, instead, is to participate, by spiritual means alone, in the immeasurable plan of evolution that cosmic law designed for humankind on earth. And in their work they show no preference for special, private causes; nor will they favor any individual, not even for the purest motives.

The curious who mean to witness vulgar "miracles" shall certainly not find them here.

To be sure, the actual events connected with the work of humankind's elder Brothers often are miraculous indeed. The more wondrous their deeds, however, the more assuredly will they not be visible to mortal eyes.

≈

It is their sphere of spiritual influence that all fellow human beings enter who in their hearts are earnestly resolved to reach the highest form of spiritual development that they are able to attain in life on earth.

The purer their will—the freer from all selfish motives and desires—the more distinctly shall the Spirit's life be able to infuse them; the sooner and more strongly, too, shall they then feel that influence within.

Countless souls experience it—without suspecting its true source.

≈

CHAPTER THREE

META-PHYSICAL EXPERIENCES

Any human being may, at given times, have *meta-physical* experiences, provided there exist specific *meta-physical* conditions, and there is not too much resistance active in the physical environment. Best endowed for having such experiences are persons of the simplest disposition and—true artists: the creative geniuses whose source of inspiration lies within.

⚘

To receive within oneself a genuine creative impulse or an original idea is, in itself, a kind of meta-physical experience.

Nonetheless, there is a fundamental difference between artistic inspiration of whatever form— or the profounder kind of meta-physical perception that any person may at times be granted, and which may reach remarkable intensity in people of innate potential—and that quite singular experience of nonmaterial realities known among the few for whom the spiritual heritage of humankind is truly more than just a source to satisfy a thirst for knowledge: the spiritual helpers of humanity, who know themselves entrusted with this faculty of spiritual perception only to the end that, from the heights of sacred mountains, they might offer help and guidance to their spiritually younger fellow souls here on earth.

The few to whom I here refer are not to be confused with so-called mystics.

༄

"Mysticism" and the Royal Art entrusted to the true initiates in the dimension of the Spirit are altogether different things.

The experience of a mystic is much like that of the creative artist.

Both receive their inspiration from a sphere they do not know, and which they consciously could never enter in complete awareness of their faculties and of their personal identity.

Both feel gripped and overwhelmed by some unknown external force and, thus, become that power's voice; or they may solely witness its effect within themselves in silence.

Meta-Physical Experiences

Completely different from such experience is the situation of the true initiate: of one who has been consecrated in the realm of Spirit, as a master of the Royal Art, and who is, thus, a Son and Brother of the Luminaries, who mediate eternal Light.

For he is every moment fully conscious of his being present and alive in each of the three separate dimensions that together constitute Reality: the domain of physical matter; the dimension of the soul, whose elements are nonmaterial; and the world of radiant spiritual substance.

At no time is he in a state of ecstasy or any kind of trance, and he rejects all mystifying rituals and exercises; for otherwise he could not be a member of the spiritual Brotherhood, a Son of the immortal Fathers.

⚘

WHILE GATHERING experiences in nonmaterial dimensions, he remains completely conscious of his own identity in each of these distinct domains. His self-awareness in the world of physical perception, which is present to all mortals in their waking state is, therefore, at no time diminished in the least.

On the contrary, his perception of external matters is not only widened, but raised to the degree of clarity with which he apprehends nonphysical reality.

While he "converses" with his spiritual Brothers on a nonmaterial plane, and they in turn communicate with him, he will perceive the most minute event occurring in his physical environment as clearly and intensely as the realities one can experience only with one's spiritual senses.

His consciousness is not, in other words, contracted but, instead, expanded almost to infinity.

ಞ

MUCH OF WHAT is "spoken" in the Spirit's world, which in itself comprises countless individual domains, can never be expressed in words of any human tongue. And yet, it is communicated in a clear, intelligible "language," possessing form and rhythm, full of truth and meaning, so that it would not be impossible to find compatible equivalents in human languages. However, by such human words one never could transmit as well the *spiritual* insight allowing one to see, and at the same time comprehend, the facts of spiritual reality from every side at once.

What, consequently, he may "translate" into words of a particular human language is determined by the unique endowment of the indi-

Meta-Physical Experiences

vidual Brother, as well as by the times in which he must perform his task, and, finally, the cultural environment surrounding him on earth.

Yet, whatever he discloses will at all times be the purest truth: unclouded revelation of absolute Reality, which is forever present to the eyes of every master of the Royal Art; unaffected by the countless possibilities for errors and illusions that beset all scientific probing in the physical domain.

Intellectual speculations and philosophical bravura simply have no place in any of the worlds of spiritual substance.

For here one is not, after all, "deducing" one truth from another, as is the practice in the mental quest for knowledge, which is subject to the functions of the brain.

Within the worlds of radiant spiritual substance, all truths are present as *realities* before the eyes of the beholder.

ଔ

SEEMING CONTRADICTIONS in the disclosures of all spiritual initiates of every age and region—noted with great satisfaction by those who cannot verify the truth of such disclosures—are easily explained as the result of the specific character of meta-physical perception, which lets a person see all things at once, from every side. In revealing what he sees, however, a Mediator can only show one aspect of his insight at a time, if he would be, at least to some extent, intelligible to his fellow humans, who cannot share his manner of perception. And furthermore, he often must present realities for which there are no suitable comparisons, because the physical domain does not provide analogies for the characteristic nature of existence in the Spirit's world.

The idiomatic style and diction that a Luminary chooses for his expositions are, on the other hand, his own decision. In this he might pay homage to his former teachers, be guided by his inclinations, or influenced by the demands of literary form.

Although the heart of Asia to this day encloses, as it has through the millennia, the physical location of the Temple in which the Spirit's energies are centered here on earth, none of the Brothers who look upon this spiritual center on our planet as their true home on this earth is obligated to employ the concepts of religion and philosophy of Eastern cultures when he gives form to his disclosures.

Meta-Physical Experiences

Thus, if a member of this circle, although his roots are in the West, will nonetheless make use of Eastern terms and images, it is a matter of free choice. It may express his fondness for oriental poetry, his love of certain metaphors, which more effectively convey realities of Spirit than Western usage can and, finally, his wish to leave profound and unforgettable experiences in their authentic setting.

Even at his highest level of development a Mediator working in the world remains a human being; indeed, is grateful for his human state. He, thus, is not devoid of human inclinations, is no ascetic without feeling for this life on earth. This is a fact, however, which some fanatics of renunciation who reject all earthly things have difficulty comprehending, because they can no longer break the spell that chains them to their demon-prompted creed.

But is there any human being capable of feeling and affection who would not prefer to speak of treasured things in words once heard from kindly teachers?

༄

To be sure, the same realities could very well be rendered also in the forms of a completely different culture, without becoming any less authentic.

The only danger is "translation" of such truths by anyone not qualified.

It is more difficult than many would suspect to recreate a sentence uttered by a true initiate, within a Christian context, so that its message will be clear in India; or to recast ideas conceived in China in the specific mold of European thought.

And frequently one even must combine ideas and concepts found in very different traditions, if certain facts of spiritual reality, which still are new to Western minds, should nonetheless become intelligible to a reader in that world.

But no one seeking truth should ever be misled to think that by such free employment of the means of presentation the writer is intending to promote the doctrines of religion and philosophy from whose particular vocabulary he adopted whatever proved most useful to evoke an understanding of eternal truth.

⁂

It is well known that social groups who aim to guide their members to transcendent, nonmaterial goals observe the custom of giving up the proper names of their constituents and of addressing them, within that circle, by other chosen names.

Meta-Physical Experiences

The following will shed some light on the true origin of this tradition, which may be traced to humankind's beginnings.

One also might be mindful in this context of these verses from the Book of Genesis:

"Neither shall thy name any more be called Abram, but thy name shall be Abraham."

And, similarly, "Thy name shall not be called any more Jacob, but Israel shall be thy name."

※

THE PROPER name borne by an individuated spiritual self is something very different from the extraneous appellation given human beings by tradition, in the language of their native land, and commonly depending on external factors.

Human mortals, too, are spiritual individualities; but—excluding rare exceptions, who can be found in every age—they are not conscious of their timeless name.

Only when the mortal being has gained consciousness of its true spiritual form and substance will it also know its timeless proper name.

Clearly, then, the spiritual proper name of any true initiate—in the past it often was a well-kept secret, as one feared it might be desecrated by being on everyone's lips—is not some arbitrary designation, as is the name a person uses in daily life, which owes its form to either an ancestral residence, or to a trade or quality of distant forebears and, lastly, also to the parents' pleasure.

Once accepted as a spiritual Son and Brother, the initiate is given his eternal name by the immortal Elders of the Brotherhood. Formed in the letter-language used among them here on earth, that name expresses the specific energies that are effective in the Brother's spiritual self.

The active power of a spiritual name is borne, however, by certain letters it contains. Its bearer, thus, could also have a different name, so long as the effective letters, which constitute his cosmic "sum"—his timeless, everlasting spiritual essence—are present in that name.

The name eternally existing in the Spirit's world is, consequently, always covered still by a protective veil, which thereby is itself already hallowed. No one, however, can pronounce a spiritual proper name—even when knowing its active letters—except the one whose self is signified within that name.

In his eternal name a Mediator is a Word within the Word of the Beginning, which speaks itself through him, who thus becomes its self-articulation in an individuated, spiritually conscious form.

※

SCIENTIFIC METHODS of research for probing into spiritual realities are, understandably, as foreign to the members of the Brotherhood on earth as to their spiritual Fathers, who never knew the Fall from the dimension of eternal Light.

The "knowledge" mastered by a true initiate, who is anointed in the Spirit, does not consist in things discovered and accumulated by his mind; it is rather the result of his possessing certain sacred faculties permitting him to apprehend, directly and at will, the object *in itself* that he intends to know.

Whatever knowledge of this world he may have gathered, by his mental faculties, becomes irrelevant for his activity and only in the rarest cases is it found compatible with spiritual reality.

The more of all such knowledge he had earlier possessed, the harder was it for him then—at the beginning of his path, when he was still his master's pupil—to overcome the obstacles imposed by preconceptions of the mind; obstacles that one must have surmounted, however, before one is initiated in the Spirit.

One must not ask for rational explanations if one would undergo this schooling, which in the end will open—to those who earned the right to enter—the inner gate which no amount of formal learning can unlock.

※

No TRUE initiate will ever be the founder of any system of dogmatic faith or esoteric "science."

Events of spiritual reality are manifested clearly to his eyes; and all his teaching deals with only this reality, which no mere system of religion or philosophy could ever comprehend.

Wherever systems of that kind infringe on spiritual realities, they merely are derivative ideas of others: of minds who seized upon the revelations made by one who had attained his knowledge through himself *becoming* the reality he sought to comprehend.

Self-styled "explorers of higher dimensions" who would impress the world by draping the results of their "research" in scientific garb are not,

Meta-Physical Experiences

of course, to be mistaken for authentic spiritual initiates.

All such "researchers" in the realm of the occult are no more than unwitting thralls of self-induced hallucinations, caused by a highly treacherous, potentially destructive faculty in human mortals; this power can be forcefully awakened, and then will let its hapless victim see, as tangible reality, all things the person's mind had earlier provided as a pattern, by means of wishes, thoughts, and fears.

Thus came into being all those bizarre "excursions on higher planes" with their description of "higher worlds" to which now more than a few "researchers of the spirit" and "esoteric teachers of secret knowledge" owe their reputation as inspired "seers" among their trusting followers. But even here one would have to examine first how much is simply purposeful invention, which as a rule is fairly easy to detect.

Given that the images of self-induced hallucination are readily transferred from soul to soul by mutual infection, the followers and pupils of such "prophets" and initiators of new sects feel sure that they have spiritual proof as to the truth of their great teachers' "revelations," as soon as they succeed, through a mystifying secret schooling, to project their own creations into the consciousness of their disciples; just like skillful hypnotists will let their subjects see, and personally experience, whatever the hypnotists desire.

Once a person has been victimized by such delusions, any later rescue is virtually impossible.

Countless souls have thus unwittingly deceived themselves, uncounted others ended as pathetic victims of betrayal.

༝

IF I DISCUSS these matters here in plain, unvarnished terms, while dealing with the nature of nonphysical experiences, I do so only to provide all honest seekers after truth with the criteria they need for forming valid judgments.

I speak of things one need not shroud in mystery and, at the same time, must shed light on others that have to be disclosed—for the sake of all those seeking Truth as spiritual Reality.

May these words not have been written here in vain!

May every reader come to understand that none among the few possessing conscious life within the Spirit's radiant substance would ever dream of so degrading the wisdom of eternal Light, which he discovers to his fellow humans, that he might stoop to "proving" spiritual realities by "scientific" methods.

The teachings of a true initiate—of one who is initiated in the realm of Spirit—are given to be verified by dedicated action in one's life.

The message he delivers to his younger fellow souls—the men and women of his time, and those of future generations—is not to be dissected intellectually, but should instead become the reader's own experience, so that the many souls that seek may find their way into the Spirit, their way to timeless Truth.

❧

CHAPTER FOUR

THE INNER JOURNEY

Aᴌᴌ ɢʀᴇᴀᴛ ɢᴏᴀʟs ɪɴ ʟɪꜰᴇ ɴᴇᴇᴅ ꜰᴀɪᴛʜ and courage.

Before you suffered on the "cross" you cannot celebrate your "resurrection."

Before you learned to summon faith, the "fiery pillar" cannot guide your foot "on dry land through the midst of the sea."

※

Tʜᴇʀᴇ sᴛɪʟʟ is much in you today that you will have to overcome, and even more you must in future learn to master if you are truly to move forward on your way.

The sea will threaten to devour you and in the desert you shall search for food in vain. Yet you must never let timidity and doubt detain you even for a moment if you have once resolved to enter on this inner path, which is to take you to yourself and, in your self, to your eternal Living God.

How difficult this is you will discover only on the way itself.

But do not be afraid!

For on this inner journey you are not alone.

All those are by your side who went that way before you.

They, too, had once to face and overcome all dangers.

Not one of them had found the journey any easier than it will be for you.

But now they have ascended to the "promised land."

They now have reached the end of all their labors and, from sacred mountains, are sending you support and inner strength.

※

FROM THE DOMAIN of those who, in their God's most radiant light, are unified as One, a single, everlasting sun of suns—beings that, in godlike splendor, illuminate all suns and worlds within creation—down to those abiding here on earth unseen, in spiritual form and, finally, the Mediators, who still experience life as mortals: through this eternal hierarchy descending, the Spirit's radiant current flows through all infinity; uniting, in sublime identity of will, all those that manifest its power.

But on the lowest rung of this eternal "Jacob's ladder," the level nearest you in life on earth, there you will find the inner helpers who can offer you their hand, provided that you want their guidance.

They shall abandon none of those who strive to make their way through all the horrors of the night, searching for the peaceful, radiant sanctuary in which their Living God is to be born —from light to light—within their timeless soul.

Do not expect, however, that their help will reach you from without; for they shall be connected with you *in yourself*, as soon as you courageously begin your inner way. Your way shall be the same which any soul that ever found its Living God has had to journey. The inner guides, who now are helping you, have also gone that way in their own day, even though their spiritual self and essence had long before been carefully prepared, for thousands of years, in order to endow them with the power to perceive and clearly comprehend all spiritual reality.

Unless your guide be one of them, he cannot ever lead you to your goal, no matter what astounding feats or miracles he elsewhere might perform.

※

You will encounter many teachers who are false; teachers who themselves need sorely to be taught, and numberless conceited braggarts will flaunt their "knowledge" to impress you.

Also, you may come upon self-righteous "holy ones" who are consumed with vanity and count it as a worthy deed to see that others are seduced to honor their pretended "holiness" and "dignity."

Again, you may be startled by outlandish pseudo-priests, seeking to bewilder anyone they can attract with the mysterious glitter of the magic symbols which, in their delusion, they stitched in imitation gold on their magician's costume.

And if you should be careless even once, you also may quite easily get caught in sundry hidden snares, which few are able to escape again unharmed who once had been entangled.

The Inner Journey

Only being constantly alert can keep you safe from danger.

❧

BEWARE OF all whose so-called wisdom touching God is taught and learned like any other subject studied by the human mind.

Beware of all who would seduce you by displaying occult powers.

There truly still are many things which even in this self-assured, supposedly "enlightened" age might strike you as a "miracle." Nor is there any doubt that wondrous faculties lie hidden deep in human nature. But never could the Spirit of Eternity so utterly mistrust its own reality that it would stoop to "proving" its existence by performing public "miracles." If some mysterious faculties reveal themselves in a particular person, it proves no more than that such faculties exist. It is no proof whatever that their owner has awakened in the Spirit as a conscious being and, therefore, can bear witness to eternal Truth, whose source is spiritual Reality.

Authentic witness of the truth is only proved by virtue of the miracle of spiritual awakening, which final truth is able to effect within the human soul. Therefore, you should not regard as truth whatever is not borne out by your innermost experience; provided you fulfill the spiritual conditions on which all such experience depends.

Forget as well the foolish notion that by consuming only certain foods, or by engaging in some foolish exercise, you might just eat or breathe yourself onto a "higher plane of spiritual life."

The Mediators of the light that shines through all creation shall never tell you to employ such means.

Nor shall they ever ask you to withdraw from life among your fellow humans, so that you might indulge in secret, mind-deluding practices or esoteric rites.

They never shall invest you with arcane "degrees," strange-sounding titles, or especial "honors," which merely would abet your vanity and kindle foolish pride.

Only what is manifest in you as spiritual *reality* —because your own endeavor made it so—has any value in their eyes and it alone will tell them where you stand.

The Inner Journey

To be sure, you will not find these Mediators holding forth from rostrums, imitating actors of the stage, nor in the market place surrounded by large crowds.

Rather, they shall offer you their help in words that you may weigh within your soul, in quiet, when you are by yourself, not swayed by cunning rhetoric.

Their help will reach you in your soul, and they shall never seek to show themselves in person.

⸎

YOU NEED not recognize the Spirit's Mediators, if in this life you ever were to meet one.

Nor is it necessary that you find them in their mortal form.

It is they who shall be finding you, and they know how to help you, even if you cannot fathom who that helper is.

Truly, they have other means of reaching you than do the vain impostors who seek to lure their flock with hints of hidden mysteries and ringing, hollow phrases.

Nor shall they ever ask for, or expect, that you pay money for their guidance; indeed, they all would rather give you their last penny than take from you so much as half a penny for their help.

What they have to bestow are treasures of the Spirit, and none who has the power to bestow such gifts would ever trade them for material things.

Only work that needs the tool of a material body may justly ask for payment in material coin.

※

Let all readers who have eyes to see and ears to hear protect themselves against pied pipers and deceivers.

They will not find it difficult to see through their disguises.

The Spirit's Luminaries, who mediate eternal Light, are not, by contrast, quite so easy to identify.

You scarcely will detect them among your fellow mortals in this life, and nothing strange or special will betray them to your eyes; for they prefer to live in undisturbed obscurity.

Compelled to live amidst the turmoil of this world, they will be indistinguishable from all other honorable persons who go about their daily tasks.

Wise are those who put their trust in them!

※

BUT NOW, my friend, who would discover truth, let us withdraw to find a quiet place, and I will show you the beginning of your way.

Collect your thoughts and listen to my words; for surely, you are now sufficiently instructed to bring an open mind to what I further have to tell you.

※

BEFORE ALL else, my friend, who would find truth, you will have to forget and clear your mind of many things that you were taught.

Your teachers filled your head with false ideas of "God," and thus destroyed in you, with baseless doctrines, the living seed from which should have arisen, out of your soul's most hallowed waters, the "lotus flower" in whose blossom shall be born the Light that is to shine in you forever.

The Spirit that "hovered over the face of the waters" pervades all reaches of infinity, but you can only find that Spirit—in yourself.

Only if it will create and form itself *in you*—as light from light—and thus become *your* God, can you bear witness to its silent wonders.

Those who seek to "comprehend" the Spirit's measureless infinity are very much deceived.

They haughtily assume their thoughts define the One whom all dimensions of creation do not grasp, and fail to see that they construed a mental phantom by whose power they are now possessed.

⁕

But we would once more sow today the seed of that eternal lotus flower in your heart.

Perhaps your soul will now provide the soil it needs to grow and flourish.

The day on which its blossom shall have fully opened, the self-begetting, self-sustaining Spirit of Eternity shall finally descend upon your soul and thus be *born* in you: to be your Living God—the God who lives within you.

Before you have experienced this, you do not know of God.

⁕

The Inner Journey

DISTRUST ALL those who tell you of a God they see in visions, a God one finds in ecstasy and trance.

Whatever can be found that way is but a phantom image of the inner world.

You still have no idea what treasures you possess within your soul's immense horizon.

One here encounters *energies* and *forces* which you would worship on your knees—like the prophet when he faced the burning bush—if I could make you see them with your eyes.

Your soul is like an ocean, vast beyond all measure, and none has ever probed its depth, nor witnessed all the wonders of the energies that form this timeless sea.

※

YOU THINK your soul to be a kind of insubstantial "body" in which you will find nothing but yourself.

Yet in reality, your soul is like an ocean, composed of countless individual drops, each possessed of latent power: or like a cloud, alive with myriads of dynamic elements—and you are to assert yourself as lord and master of this host of forces.

Unless they clearly recognize you as their master, they will benumb you with their awesome powers and you will find yourself their slave.

Once you have subdued them to your will, they must be at your service, but if misplaced humility should make you kneel before them, their mystifying energies shall never cease deluding you.

They need a will of strong resolve, a will that shall unite them all within itself.

Before you have united them within a single will, you cannot in your soul attain that state of inner quiet which alone will cause the lotus flower to develop and to blossom.

⁂

Nor shall your soul's inherent faculties allow you any sooner to perceive within yourself that silent realm of spirits, which you may sense and feel, and sometimes even see and hear—once your soul is unified within a single will—because that realm abides in you, as it does everywhere, by virtue of the selfsame energies.

Nor can the one who guides you from the realm of Spirit any sooner offer you a lucid sign, nor shall you any earlier perceive within yourself the

The Inner Journey

Spirit's timeless rulers, the Luminaries, who mediate eternal Light.

If, therefore, you would find what you are seeking, you must above all else develop in yourself a clearly formed and steadfast will, determined to assert your self.

You must be able to accept yourself if, in the Spirit's world, you seek acceptance by the Spirit.

You cannot find yourself, nor your eternal Living God, except within your inmost self.

∞

ENDEAVOR CALMLY to assert your inmost self within you, with quiet joy and with serene detachment, and turn away from all the images your still not self-collected, easily excited mind would force on your attention.

You need first to become profoundly conscious of your inmost self, secure in confidence and inner joy.

Before you have collected all your inner energies, securing your own confines on all sides—like an ocean self-defining its own shores, or like a cloud that wills its proper shape—you shall in vain endeavor to possess your soul, because its elements will only bow to someone truly worthy of their homage.

Do not assume, however, that you might ever reach this goal by shunning all activity in outer life.

As a mortal born into this world of matter, you here must strive to be productive day by day; even as nature herself, of which you now are part, never ceases to create new life and forms. Thus only shall you see your will grow strong as steel, so that your soul's dynamic forces can obey it.

There is no single thing so small or unimportant in this outer life that you could not regard it as a lesson.

There is something to be learned in every moment you experience, and no activity or work is so ignoble in itself that it might not still teach you something new.

❧

ABOVE ALL else, however, you must learn to gather and control your passing thoughts, and have them concentrate themselves on one thing at a time.

The Inner Journey

Neither a hermit's life in the desert, nor living among the wild beasts of the jungle could prove more beneficial to your goal than will the commerce in a busy city in which you are pursuing your own work.

When you have learned to not become distracted even in the loudest turmoil of this outer life; when you have gained complete control of all your thinking and your will; when your wishes only come and go as you would have them come and leave you—then only should you make the first attempt to unify within yourself the elements that form your timeless soul.

Even then you may expect to face much opposition in yourself.

Although your will is now already formed and strengthened, you still may be asserting it in vain—for quite some time—in order to subdue the many elements within your soul that are reluctant to obey it.

Each element within your soul shall struggle to possess your will alone and by itself, and none shall readily become your will's possession.

You shall more clearly understand this once you recognize that every element found in your soul

—although you think of them as innate qualities of your own nature, inseparable from yourself—is, in reality, an independent, conscious *being* in the ocean of the soul; a *being* that is driven by the will to manifest itself alone, even if it were at the expense of all the other elements within you.

But you must never feel discouraged in this continuing and often still unequal struggle to impose your will upon the many other wills that only want to manifest *themselves* within your soul.

You never must lose faith in your own powers.

And never must you lose your inner joy, nor your dispassionate serenity.

All your struggles now are but a constant test, both of your patience and of the strength you have already gained in practicing your will.

Be assured, however, that in this way you shall prevail and triumph in the end.

※

THE DAY WILL come when you shall truly feel the joy of victory in every fiber of your being.

Then shall the "lotus flower's" seed have opened, and on the Temple's sacred pond, forever hidden from the sight of mortals, the inner eye of your

The Inner Journey

invisible protector—in former days one knew him as the human being's *guardian angel*—shall see a bud upon the motionless, mysterious waters.

Full of joy he then shall call his Brothers, and from that day will chosen guardians protect the hallowed waters of your soul.

A "miracle" has here become reality.

A miracle, accomplished by a mortal. For, truly, it is easier to "hold a raging elephant by no more than a string of hemp, and guide him through a market's busy crowd" than fully to unite, within a single human will, the countless *wills* that form a human soul.

༄

But now the light of day must softly bathe the flower's bud, that it may one day bloom in all its splendor.

Trees of ageless majesty surround the mystery-enshrouded pond, protecting the still tender plant against the searing arrows of the sun, which at this time would only wither and destroy the barely sprouted seed.

The Temple's mighty walls fend off the burning sandstorms from the desert.

Now, my friend who seeks the Truth, you will have to pursue a new activity.

But this new task indeed requires also outer calm and time for meditation.

You will be able to devote yourself to this, however, after you have finished with your daily chores, or in the peace and quiet of the early morning.

You now must learn how to give voice to inner questions, quietly and calmly, and then to listen for an answer in yourself.

You cannot be too silent as you pursue this task.

What still abides concealed within your depth, but soon shall be revealed, cannot be heard while noisy thoughts are rushing through your mind.

It speaks within your heart of hearts, but you can still not hear its word, because its voice is fainter than the call of a bird far in the distance.

Be very careful, lest it shy away.

Pay close attention even to its faintest sound.

Its voice in you can easily be missed if you will not keep perfect silence.

The Inner Journey

At first your inner questions will be answered in a voice so faint that even a breath in your soul would scatter its sound to the winds.

One day, however, you shall truly learn to hear that inner voice, and will be able to distinguish it from any other voice that you might hear within you.

You will not hear the Spirit's voice the way your ear perceives external sounds.

Nor will you hear it speaking in your native tongue, nor in any other language spoken on this earth.

Yet what that voice shall have to tell you will be far more intelligible to your understanding than anything you ever heard from childhood on in words of any human tongue.

༄

From here on you will have to follow the counsels of that inner voice.

All future progress on your inner way will henceforth be determined only by your loyalty.

Step by step you will begin to recognize how your own will no longer serves you merely as your mortal insight wishes, but that, instead, you can already redirect it, almost imperceptibly, according to the Spirit's will, whose guidance you are given through that voice.

More and more deeply shall you penetrate into your soul's profoundest mysteries.

The more you may already comprehend, the greater mysteries you still shall fathom, hidden in dimensions unrevealed.

With gratitude receive and carefully preserve even the smallest insight that your soul will grant you; for if you gratefully accept what may seem little, you will the soonest know the full abundance of experience.

In the end you shall behold a realm of inner wonders of which no human words today could give you the faintest conception.

Events shall happen in your life which you today would call impossible, and such they truly are —today.

But the most astounding of all wonders, it will then appear to you, is that so much power should be granted *you*; for now you need no longer wait in anxious doubt to see your deepest longing answered, because it henceforth shall fulfill itself: by virtue of its own inherent power.

The Inner Journey

IF YOU HAVE thus far always loyally fulfilled the expectations of your inner guidance, the lotus flower on the sacred pond within the Spirit's temple shall slowly have unfolded more and more.

It now shall not be long before you see the day on which the fully opened blossom will shine upon the waters in a light whose radiance is not of this material earth.

Know, then, my friend, who would find truth, that you have come to see the day on which the Will of God reveals itself—as your own Living God—in your eternal self.

As God is *born* in you, so are you *born* in God.

What here is done remains a mystery which even those who have awakened in the Spirit do not see.

❧

TO BE SURE, you cannot yet forgo your inner guide; but you will henceforth be united with him in a different way.

Already when the lotus bud has surfaced on the waters, it may be that you will behold your inner guide before you in a nonmaterial image, provided you possess the faculty one needs for such perception.

What you shall thus behold, however, is not your inner guide himself.

It rather is a likeness of his person, molded by his will from certain "plastic" energies within your soul.

Be grateful if your inner guide is able to be near you in this way; if he can teach you through his likeness, so that you feel as if you heard his voice.

Yet do not be concerned if in this life you never see your teacher's likeness face to face.

Only in exceptional cases can he thus appear to you in visual form, and he never shall approach you in this way if it might cause you any harm, or tempt you to misuse your soul's potential for the sake of seeing other things.

It is better for you never to behold your teacher's likeness than to risk that his influence upon the elements that form your soul might also render them susceptible to forces that deceive.

If, thus, you do not *see* your inner guide, you will the more securely *feel* his presence in your heart; and what your eyes may not perceive without, shall manifest itself the more concretely to your inmost comprehension.

※

Now, HOWEVER, that your God is born in you, as you are born in God, your inner guide shall manifest himself within you only in his spirit's highest life: united with your inmost self and with the voice of your eternal Living God.

Whenever he is with you, it will appear to you as though your consciousness and his were only one.

He shall no longer guide you by his teachings, but rather open up to you his very self; and from the treasures of his inner life you will select and make your own whatever you still need.

Above all this, however, the joy of God will shine in sun-like splendor, and what you once had suffered in your quest for light and knowledge, before you found your inner way, shall now seem like the torments of the damned that you had lived through long ago.

Before your eyes expanding you behold eternity, whose farthest depth will make you fathom ever deeper realms, feeling certain in the knowledge that, united with your Living God, you will proceed from mystery to mystery forever without end.

If you observe yourself amidst the joys and sorrows of this earthly life, you still shall only see a mortal—and yet, your spirit, radiant in your Living God, shall be exalted far above all physical mortality; for now your soul is made a kingdom in the spheres of the eternal, a heaven in the realm of heavens.

❧

This, then, is the inner way, my friend, that you will have to choose and follow to the end, if you would truly find your Living God.

The way to God is in you—within your very self!

No other way shall ever lead you to your highest goal: to your awakening within the kingdom of the Spirit.

If you do not awaken in that realm while you still live your life on earth, you will continue sleeping, for a long time, also in your life beyond, when you have left this mortal world. Eternities may pass before one in that other life can finally awaken you: from dreams which you yourself brought into being and which may then enslave your consciousness for aeons.

❧

The Inner Journey

Now let me also offer you the following advice:

Once you have decided to pursue your inner way, you shall be needing a resilient "staff" that will support you on your journey.

You shall not lack the proper "wood" to fashion such a staff if in yourself you can detect and feel the latent energy contained in words, such as it manifests itself in every human language.

Find some words that touch your heart; words by which you feel inspired, stirred, and inwardly uplifted.

Set aside a little time each day and, if you can, at always the same hour; a time when you may seek to penetrate the spirit of such words in contemplation and will not be disturbed by duties of your daily life.

Continue using such a word that moved you, in your daily contemplation, and let it be an exercise to school your thinking for some time to come; much as a player on the flute repeats the same phrase many times, until it gains its purest sound.

You will find many words throughout this book that lend themselves to such an exercise in thinking.

More I gave you in my other books.

To be sure, you are not obligated to confine yourself to words included in my texts.

The sacred writings of humanity are rich in words that may inspire and uplift your soul.

Sages and poets have given the world such words in abundance.

The only danger you incur by using words from other sources is that you also will absorb the error-laden doctrines which lack of insight and conventional interpretation will lead you to read into those words.

Thus, I would advise you, at least in the beginning, rather to select your words from books I wrote; given that you are resolved to trust me with your guidance.

Begin, then, as I already told you, by searching with your mind for the profoundest meaning of the words you chose.

Next, however, try to find a way of thinking without "words."

Do not give up until you feel assured that—through this wordless comprehension—you have completely grasped the deepest meaning of those words.

The Inner Journey

At the same time, write the words in your own hand, clearly, and apart from others, by themselves. And let your eyes create an image of them that you can retain.

Now try to feel the words you chose as if they were your own.

Seek thereafter to create within yourself the spiritual consciousness that moved their author to express those words.

Try to awaken your sense of *inner hearing* by listening for the sound those words produce within you.

When you are certain that you have achieved results in all these forms of comprehending, you will be ready to proceed—but only then, even if you do not reach this point for quite some time.

※

I MUST EXPRESSLY warn you: do not take this admonition lightly and proceed too soon!

To be sure, you well may think that all this can be easily accomplished in the space of a few hours.

Perhaps, indeed, you feel already certain, even as you are receiving these instructions, that you no longer really need to practice such a way of comprehending.

Many who had once intended to pursue their inner goal fell by the wayside—at the very start—because they held that view.

There is far more demanded here than you at first are likely to suspect.

But often one must speak of things that are profoundly different by using terms that, on the surface, seem to be quite similar.

Thus, you here need not possess what one might call an "ear for language," although a person who intuitively senses the rhythm, sound, and inner weight of words is not too far from understanding what the present task demands.

But if you truly have accomplished everything that is required, you shall have gained a new and much expanded sense of your existence, a far more conscious way of living your external life; and this will give you the assurance that you are safe from any form of self-deception.

Then, my friend, who seeks the highest of all human goals, you may continue on your way.

You now must try to feel those words within yourself, with your entire being.

The Inner Journey

Those words must now begin to come alive in you.

Not just your soul should now be penetrated by the spirit of those words, but all your body must begin to feel them: in its every fiber.

With yourself, your soul, and your whole body must those words now be completely fused into a single consciousness.

Your mortal body must become the very body of those words, as if no other life were active in its form.

The elements that shape your soul, already integrated fully with your will, must now be also integrated with the words you chose; and you must feel yourself as if you were the very consciousness alive within those words.

With the attainment of this goal you have accomplished something great.

For the first time you shall here encounter Life itself: the energy that is alive in you and in all living things.

It will appear to you as if you had awakened on a new and different earth, within a world you never dreamed existed.

You shall perceive and comprehend that the condition mortals call their "waking state" is in effect a deep, lethargic sleep and muddled dream.

※

ALREADY HERE you may begin to see the Spirit's world with clarity, provided that your innate faculties allow for such perception and, owing to your nature, your strength lies more in visual than in conceptual experience.

But if your faculties are such that you can only apprehend what you would know if you are able conceptually to grasp it, then you will not so much *behold* as rather *comprehend* the insights you receive.

In either case, however, you now shall have become a new and very different being; for you have gained a consciousness of your own self to which your present sense of being can hardly be compared.

For even as a little oil lamp's flicker will vanish in the radiant sun at noon, so too shall be absorbed and vanish, in a new and different consciousness, what you today still call your "self-awareness."

The Inner Journey

You then will understand the reason why an ancient sage once spoke of life as of the "light of men"; and you will comprehend the depth of the majestic words that have inspired so much commentary:

"In the beginning is the Word, and the Word is with God, and God is the Word.

"In it all things have life, and its life is the light of men.

"And the light shines in the darkness, and the darkness cannot put it out."

❧

THE AUTHOR of those words knew very well what he was saying, and so shall you, when you have reached that threshold on your way.

But remember, "the kingdom of heaven submits to force, and only the forceful shall seize it."

Without controlling your impatience, without untiring practice of your inner faculties, you cannot rightfully expect success.

Yet do not think that stubborn, blind exertion or convulsive strain might ever bring you closer to your goal.

For that is not the meaning of this admonition.

You must at all times feel surrounded by an atmosphere of quiet joy and of dispassionate serenity, and all your care must be directed toward attaining, with utmost sensitivity, the keen perceptiveness within yourself of which I spoke above.

You need more "force" to curb your passions in this way than you should want for some heroic deed, conspicuous for all the world to see.

If, however, you have carefully considered what I told you, and will in future undertake what is required, then I can offer you assurance that also you shall one day find yourself among those granted to perceive, within themselves, the mystery of "the kingdom of heaven."

ை

BEGIN, THEN, your demanding inner journey!

May never-failing patience accompany your efforts to the end!

Help and guidance from above shall always be beside you.

Do not look back upon the life that is behind you: the past with all its joys and sorrows, its good deeds and its wrongs.

The Inner Journey

Also bear in mind that for your task it is of no importance whether you have mastered all the learning of this world, or whether you rank last among the uninstructed.

Do not attempt to live in separation from your fellow human beings, nor ever think that you might benefit by choosing an eccentric way of life, cultivating habits that ignore the customs of your time and place.

Even less important for your inner journey shall be what you eat and drink; for nothing here can either help or harm you, as long as it will keep your body in good health.

If you prefer avoiding the meat of slaughtered animals, by all means, do avoid it; and if you would abstain from wine, then simply do not drink it; but you ought never to imagine that such a choice will make of you a "purer," let alone a "morally superior," human being.

The same is to be said concerning physical passion between man and woman.

Let not your drives reduce you to the level of a brute, but always keep them firmly tamed, that they may never vanquish you against your will and render you their slave. Yet do not blasphemously scorn a mystery that you can only comprehend in all its purity when you yourself shall have awakened in the Spirit.

Not without having probed the very depth of Being did priests of ancient cults declare the symbols representing procreation to be sacred. And, truly, what they venerated here was more than just an image of nature's inexhaustible fertility.

Abstention is demanded only where the untamed passion of your drives might lead to harm, both to yourself and others.

Abstention is demanded from all vices, because they soon would stifle and, in the end, extinguish your lofty striving toward the Spirit.

Avoid all things that might bring harm to others, or yourself.

You even should avoid all heartless thoughts!

Feel love for your own self! For if you cannot love your very self, you will show little kindness for another if you but "love your neighbor like yourself."

Pursue the path that you have chosen, but also let all others follow theirs; even should their goals lie far behind your own.

The Inner Journey

You do not know when others' time has come, and thus you have no right to interrupt their sleep.

Do not imagine that you could awaken them; for none of them escape their sleep before their time has come.

But if their hour is approaching, then they themselves shall ask you to instruct them.

Only then are you allowed to speak of what you know.

And only then shall your assistance also be effectively supported by the Luminaries, who mediate eternal Light.

You are not called upon to guide another to the Spirit, from within the Spirit's realm, and those entrusted with that calling shall never pressure anyone to follow and accept their guidance.

Set out, then, on your inner path to your own self, in quiet joy and confidence.

The way to your own self shall take you to your inner guide, in the domain of your eternal soul, and he shall lead you, in yourself, to your sublimest goal.

Your way to your own self is, in the end, your way to God.

For never shall you know of God unless you find your Living God's true Being—within your inmost self.

※

But now I want to tell you also more of other things, which will enable you to understand the workings of the Spirit's world on earth, as well as other hidden laws—if, indeed, it is your honest will to know the Spirit's ways.

I shall adorn your house with festive garlands.

Garlands braided out of flowers I collected on my highest paths, and at my final journey's end, within my blossoming garden.

Do not despoil those garlands, but leave each flower where you find it.

For otherwise you will not grasp, in undistorted clarity, the one great Truth which every sentence of this book would make you see.

And then you might not comprehend the mystery that here reveals itself in silent words: the mystery of Life divine in mortals—the mystery that is the Living God.

※

CHAPTER FIVE

THE EN-SOF

THE EN-SOF—THE INFINITE, EXISTING OF itself—is Spirit, which in itself encloses everything that is.

The forces of the universe, by contrast, work as causes generating numerous *effects*; and this misled you to pursue the quest for an imagined *first*, or *primal* cause.

Yet there has never been a "first cause" of the kind that you envision.

God eternally brings forth God's Self, rising from the chaos of the unformed elements of Being.

Nothing here is "cause," nor anything "effect."

There is alone the Spirit's free, self-knowing *will*, which manifests its very being, for itself, as *God*.

At their very source, where they are hurled forth from the Ground of Being, the unformed elements of Being manifest themselves as chaos, as the profoundest, most prolific forces of eternal nature.

They here assert themselves as purely driven needs and urges, without awareness of their being, nor of the consequences they effect.

They here still are opposed to one another, and every element asserts itself alone.

But from the self-assertion of opposing elements there will result *polarity* and, thus, reciprocal attraction; and such attraction will prepare, in time not countable in human terms, the gradual accumulation of the scattered elements.

In the dimension of the soul of mortal humans the elements arising from the Ground of Being will then become united once again: if human will aspires to attain that goal.

The turmoil in your heart that seeks expression; the inner restlessness that keeps you constantly in motion; the driving need of having to achieve a certain goal: herein you may perceive the influence effected by the elements of Being, which

The En-Sof

seek to unify themselves again in you, and now in a specific, individuated form.

༄

TODAY, HOWEVER, there still are many of these elements competing in you for your will. In the sublime, developed form your consciousness requires, they manifest themselves within you as the energies that form your timeless soul.

Today, you do not yet command the dominating will that can unite all of these energies within you.

What you today regard as your own *self*, both in your inner life and in the world without, is seldom more than only one among the countless wills that one day shall be unified within the radiant spiritual scintilla that is your consciously awakened self.

For only in a conscious self can God's eternal consciousness reveal itself anew: manifested by the elements born in the Ground of Being.

Rising from the horrifying turmoil in the lowest depth of nature, both in its visible and its unseen dimension, until they reach their integration in the conscious self-awareness of a mortal born on earth—and there are countless "earths" inhabited by human mortals—the elements at work within the Ground of Being will once again ascend to their sublimest height: returning to a new and conscious life in God.

The physical phenomena your senses can observe, and which you speak of as "forces of nature," are in fact no more than visible *effects*: reflections showing the reciprocal exchange and influence between the elements of Being, but not in any way identical with these eternal elements.

What you regard as the "reality" of the observable—as well as of the unseen—universe is ultimately "real" only insofar as it represents the *effect* created by the elements that underlie the Ground of Being, made manifest at various levels of activity and form.

The universe *exists* because the elements of Being cause it to exist; not, however, "of itself."

༶

You still are speaking of a "God" whom you consider the "creator" of all things; a "God" who brought forth and sustains an everlasting world in "His" own honor, declaring "His" own glory.

Yet such a view of God and of creation's origin could only be excused in ages of the past that

The En-Sof

still possessed no knowledge of the countless ways in which the elements of Being manifest themselves; knowledge that should be sufficient for a thinking mind today to put away the old ideas.

Clinging to them in this day and age is at the same time blasphemy and folly.

God is the creator of only God's own Self in all things that *exist*: and everything that truly *is* embodies Being that is God's.

God brings forth God's Self alone, and did not, as you believe, create the human being and the world.

❧

THE FORCES that give shape to all the suns and worlds within creation are aspects of the Spirit —elements that form the Ground of Being—and as they manifest themselves in time and space, they generate phenomena within these limitations: things existing only for a time, and always subject to the laws of space.

New elements, however, are continuously hurled forth from the Ground of Being, while others are unceasingly returning to their source.

Thus it was since time began, and so it shall remain for all eternity.

Forever alternating their effect, the elements that form the Ground of Being at times will manifest themselves as forces that create, at other times again they will destroy what they created.

They themselves, however, simply *are in being* —from eternity to eternity—although forever changing their effect, and they were not "created," as it were, by anyone.

❦

THERE NEVER has been a "beginning" of this everlasting Life, nor can it ever have an "end."

The whole, unfathomable universe with its immeasurable wealth of forms, with all its visible and its unseen dimensions, is but the ever restless surface of an eternal spiritual sea from which arises, through its own inherent power, the radiant cloud of Godhead.

Except for *God*, there would exist no universe; and if there were no universe, there would exist no *God*.

The *perpetuum mobile*, which fools and sages endeavored to invent, always has existed and cannot be "invented," in that sense, a second time.

The En-Sof

Those who labored to invent it merely sensed within themselves, albeit in minute proportions, the essence of the boundless All; the truth of that which is in being through Itself—without beginning. without end—Eternal Life proceeding through its cosmic cycles.

༄

CHAPTER SIX

ON SEEKING GOD

YOU ARE STILL SEARCHING FOR A GOD BEYOND the stars who rules in the infinity of space.

But I can tell you this:

Before your God is born in you, as you are born in God, your search shall never end.

Before your God is born in you, you shall in vain make all dimensions of creation tremble with your anguished cry for God.

༄

YOU MAY have heard it said that mortal beings are actually "Gods" in temporal disguise and merely need to discover their true nature to find themselves as "Gods" for all eternity.

Those who hold this view are very far from God, much farther than they might suspect.

Not *you* are God, but in your inmost self alone can God gain timeless form, and in such union you shall then be One, as word and meaning are combined in song.

Nothing then can ever separate you from your God in all eternity.

For God shall from this time forth be alive in you forever.

※

You should not, therefore, any longer search for God in measureless infinities, in worlds you cannot reach, behind the farthest galaxies.

As long as you are seeking God, your God is not yet born in you.

As soon as God is born in you, your search is at an end.

There is nothing so unnecessary as your "seeking God."

What you should seek instead, however, is the inner path on which your God can reach you.

Having found it, see that everything within you shall be ready and prepared for God becoming one with you.

※

COMPREHEND: THE will of the eternal, all-embracing Spirit *wills* that you exist, and it is even now alive in you, seeking one day to reveal its self-born life in you as God.

Advent, the time of preparation, should henceforth animate your soul; for, truly, you are *Bethlehem*, and in you shall be born your king: the One, the only One, who can indeed redeem you.

CHAPTER SEVEN

ON LEADING AN ACTIVE LIFE

BE ACTIVE AS YOU MAKE YOUR INNER WAY and always seek productive use of all your faculties and powers.

Having one day found your God within you, your whole existence shall be action; indeed, your very self shall then be pure activity.

❧

GOD IS A living fire!

A fire that consumes all things that idly stagnate and decay.

The Spirit's will cannot bring forth its life within you—as your Living God—if you do not pursue an active life on earth, as if you were already one with God.

❧

Your living God will be a God of energy and daring, not some demon of anemic wishes and consuming fears.

May you always love to lead an active life, even as the Spirit is itself forever active, eternally creating its own essence.

How can you hope that you and God shall ever become one, while yet your love is seeking other goals?

You cannot find yourself within your God, unless you are resolved to be united with God in a life of action; for the eternal Living God is not an idol of enraptured dreamers.

In souls alone that have awakened can God come forth in timeless form.

The Godhead's Light is far too radiant to be endured by souls that seek no more than twilight.

༶

Unify the elements that form your soul and use them for your highest goals.

Complete whatever you can finish in your life on earth and be at all times active, as far as your ability permits.

On Leading an Active Life

Thus, you one day shall be strong enough to stand before your God—before the Living God within you—without fear.

※

YOU WOULD not have existence in this life if Life, the Spirit's very action, were not, in fact, at work in you.

Nor would you have *eternal life*, but for the fact that all the Spirit's works are everlasting, even as itself.

In life on earth, however, you have existence that is only temporal, and thus it is your duty in this temporal domain to bring forth works in earthly life; even as, within the Spirit's world, your own existence is brought forth, eternally, by will of the eternal.

Only by pursuing a continuously active life can you truly prove your worth; and through your actions must you have prepared yourself, as your inner guidance shall demand, if your Living God is to be born within you.

※

CHAPTER EIGHT

ON "HOLY MEN" AND "SINNERS"

T HOSE GIVEN INSIGHT INTO FINAL THINGS have always viewed the "holy man" in his conceit and false humility as something ludicrous and foolish; they also can distinguish, however, between some unctuous hypocrite and those inspired souls that have at times been canonized.

The Spirit's guides would like to see you living proudly and with self-esteem, not as a sorry wretch who begs for mercy at the gates of heaven, not as some miserable penitent.

They want to see you turn your life into a work of art, not meekly to submit to life the way a beast of burden bears its yoke.

❦

All who will allow themselves to be deflected from their path by sins and feelings of guilt are still not worthy to attain their goal. They who would achieve the greatest of all victories must not consume themselves with anguished thoughts, seeing that the dust of daily life at times will stain their garment.

Those who constantly would cleanse their coat of every speck shall soon be losing sight of their sublimest goal.

I certainly do not suggest that one should wallow in the mud; but those who would attain their inner goal must learn to disregard the dust and all the little stains that needs will soil their garment on the way.

You never shall advance a single step, nor ever find your natural stride, if you allow some errors —which no mortal can entirely avoid—to distract you on your journey.

The so-called holy man, however, is like a person who has cut the tendons of his legs with his own hands, and now is lying by the wayside as a cripple, but dreams with open eyes that he can fly.

༺༻

Truly, I would rather see you wade through sin and guilt up to your neck than ever tempted to become a "saint."

On "Holy Men" And "Sinners"

You would be wasting your most precious energy if you attempted living like a "holy person" and sought above all else to purge yourself of "sin."

You cannot properly employ your strength if you are constantly concerned with not committing any "sin"; because wherever you are truly active, you cannot help but "sin" and make mistakes—against your will.

But as a sculptor's work is surely not diminished by the dust of marble on the floor, so also shall your timeless self, which you would carve from unhewn rock, by no means lose its value because of the debris you leave behind until you hammered out your lasting form.

Forget the workshop with its dust and rubble and always keep your mind upon the work of art you are to fashion from your present life; a work of radiant beauty and enduring without end.

※

AND IF you took a serious fall where standing firm had been your will, see that you promptly rise again and do not dwell on your defeat.

But even where your will had led you to succumb, your only thought should be to get back on your feet again at once.

Remorse will help you nothing after you have fallen—but if you rise again with strong resolve, this may prepare you to gain permanent self-confidence, which will in turn allow you to avoid recurrent falls.

Clearly, those who feel that they are strong enough to rise again if they should fall are going to advance more quickly than others, who hesitate at every step because they fear that they might stumble.

There is nothing that can harm you on your way except your fear of the obstructive energies of guilt; and these impeding forces derive their power solely from your fear.

Lead a life of kindness and compassion—free of fear—but never let compassion undermine the energies you need to keep yourself protected.

Show kindness always and to all things having life; but kindness toward the tiger is a well-aimed shot; for even what you must destroy should not be made to suffer.

※

AGAIN, YOUR kindness and compassion must be free, lest even they become your vices.

None is free but they who free themselves.

On "Holy Men" And "Sinners"

No "God" imagined by your mind beyond the stars of the external universe can ever grant you freedom.

If you, however, seek to free yourself, your God will likewise help you: your Living God, who wants to be *reborn* in you one day.

You have yourself created all the phantoms that torment you, and only you possess the power also to destroy them.

You still consider much as "sin" and "guilt" that truly does not justify such scorn; and other things you will take lightly, or even count among your "virtues," although they are temptations that might lead to your undoing.

To be sure, you should not purposely seek out temptation; yet, on the other hand, you must not, like some self-anointed "saint," be so obsessed with sin that you suspect temptations all around you.

※

Go your way with pride and self-assurance, knowing that you will be best protected if you can fully trust yourself.

No "sin" nor "fall" can then impede your stride, until the day that, strengthened by the Spirit's power, you shall attain the goal that lies within yourself.

But—heed this warning and advice:

Better suffer "sin" and "guilt," but guard against the vain ambition to be "holy."

※

CHAPTER NINE

THE HIDDEN SIDE OF NATURE

WHEN IN THE PRECEDING CHAPTERS OF this book I spoke of things *invisible*, I nearly always either meant the unseen realm that is your soul, and which unfolds by virtue of your soul's inherent energies, or the sublime dimension of the Spirit: the timeless world from which you hail and that you now must find again, if you would reach your Living God and know the inner peace which this world cannot grant you.

There is, however, still another realm of unseen things that has to be included; a realm by which your physical existence is invisibly surrounded, in much the same way as material shapes and objects are around you in the world you see.

This physically unseen dimension constitutes a part of the domain of matter that still is little known, although it is by far the larger part of physical reality.

The hidden realm of nature will at first provide your inner guide and teacher with the bridge he needs to cross whenever he would reach you; for then you are not yet prepared to recognize him in yourself—by virtue of your soul's already integrated energies—as you shall later know him: in your Living God.

Initially, he cannot reach your inner self except by way of the invisible dimensions of this world.

※

THERE ALWAYS have been people who could "see" this hidden side of nature with great clarity.

For attaining their sublimest inner goal, this faculty of "seeing" was, and is, of no significance.

Those who have that gift can simply see more things than others; as someone looking through a telescope may recognize the rings and moons of distant planets, while another, with unaided eyes, is able to distinguish only twinkling points.

The faculty of seeing the invisible domain of nature is rooted in an organ of the human being's material body; in modern times it is, however, rarely found to have enough potential for development to be of any use.

The Hidden Side of Nature

In ancient times this organ often was far more developed in humanity, and also future generations shall see it flourish once again; provided they are able to make certain that its function will no longer cause them any harm.

The evolution of such organs, which are not needed in external life, proceeds like ebb and flow, with alternating levels of intensity, within the species as a whole.

So, too, the faculty of seeing the invisible dimension of this physical, material world will often seem almost extinct, only to flare up again, at other times, in very many places.

We here are dealing with vestigial organs of the human creature body of primeval times. Still, such organs will prove beneficial only if a person's soul has been prepared to put the given faculty to proper use.

༄

INDIVIDUALS IN whom the organ for perceiving the nonvisible domain of nature is completely developed are, therefore, always equally endowed with more *experienced* souls, given that their energies had been at work on earth before, in many human lives of earlier times.

Where the faculty of "seeing" the nonvisible dimension is joined by the desire to gain higher knowledge, persons thus endowed shall not fall victim to deceptive forces in the unseen realm of nature; for they shall find compassionate guides and caring helpers from the Spirit's realm who will enhance their understanding of the things they see.

It is even possible that, once their inner selves have fully been awakened, higher beings in the Spirit's realm will grant them power over energies inherent in that unseen world, so that they may take part in the eternal plan of human beings' spiritual development, such as it has been furthered, for many thousands of years, by the Spirit's Luminaries, who mediate eternal Light.

As a rule, there are but few among the seers of the hidden realm who will prove suited for this task.

Even so, however, it is greatly to be wished that those who feel they might possess the organ for perceiving the physically invisible dimension of reality, in more or less developed form, would carefully observe that faculty and guard it well against abuse.

The Hidden Side of Nature

With proper care one might see many a potential gift become developed, which then could find much beneficial use.

The world has need of many "workers in the vineyard," and it would profit much today if it could once more find enlightened counselors and teachers capable of walking safely also on the hidden paths of nature's unseen realm.

One cannot here gain insight by experimenting with somnambulants and mediums submerged in trance, but only through the personal, direct experience of those endowed with the required organ of perception.

One surely must give credit to scientific zeal, but with psychical experiments which, as their very name implies, are based on false assumptions, given that they do not involve the *soul*, one is merely attracting parasitic forces from the invisible domain of nature.

These parasites of nature's unseen realm are creatures that, in certain ways, resemble closely the dynamic energies that form the human soul, although the two must never be confused.

To do so would be like mistaking apes, grinning and frowning between the bars that hold them in their cages, with the inspired artistry of brilliant actors representing human feelings on the stage.

※

THE CREATURES of the unseen part of nature one attracts in "para-psychical" experiments, as well as in séances, where in worshipful solemnity participants believe they are communicating with "departed souls," are not by any means devoid of a degree of consciousness, and often they "know" more than those who mean to probe their knowledge. Their self-awareness is, however, only dim and dreamlike, so that one cannot properly, by human standards, condemn them as immoral if they pretend to be whatever their interrogators think they are, or wish to find in them.

Above all else, they crave to manifest their own existence, and to that end they will resort to every means within their power; but they will also go beyond their limits, feigning to have powers they do not possess.

They are not bound by moral laws, nor by a sense of conscience.

To destroy you will afford them no less pleasure than to lend you strength, if only they can make their own existence known by means of the effect their power has on you.

Dreadful is the fate of those whom nature's unseen parasites already have within their grip.

Like leeches they will drain their victim's energies; for they must feed upon the life-blood of their prey, if mortal humans would have them at their service.

If victims cannot rid themselves by their own strength, these creatures' ghastly urges will enslave them, until their very soul shall finally have *died*, because its energies will gradually detach themselves and leave them. And when their mortal form shall one day have been laid to rest, their former consciousness will perish and return to nothing: the only true, because *eternal*, "death" that human mortals have to fear.

ॐ

VERY FEW can speak from knowledge about the phantomlike, deceitful nature of these beings, which cannot properly be named, since visible reality provides no suitable analogies.

It is the power of these unseen creatures that fakirs use to work their eerie feats; and as the world is unaware of their existence, people marvel at the fakirs' deeds, if ever there appears a true performer of that demon-ridden craft.

These beings are found capable of many things that human beings cannot ever equal, so long as they rely on merely their own physical capacities.

They "see" your thoughts more clearly than even you may know them, and the most secret things you picture in your mind they can make visible before your very eyes.

They can produce material forms and substances that, for a certain time, will be as tangible as any other thing on earth, or any substance that you know; for these invisible intelligences are the hidden weavers shaping every earthly form, and they direct the unseen threads that underlie all visible phenomena in nature.

They can assume the bodily appearances of persons who have long since died; for every form that once existed here on earth continues to be present in their sphere; namely, in a shape that one might—very loosely—speak of as a casting mold or die, from which one may at any time produce another copy.

In reality, this casting mold is an extremely delicate, invisible configuration: a system, as it were, of leaf-like membranes that preserves, in mathematically exact proportions, every inner and external part that once had formed a mortal human body.

As a rule, that die or matrix is compressed into the smallest space within itself, but under suitable conditions it will become inflated, so to speak, with the organic energies that normally sustain the physical activity and body of the medium.

During the time that such a manifestation lasts, the medium must needs be kept in the unconscious state one knows as "trance."

The inflated phantom body, which is of very brief duration even under optimum conditions, functions as the instrument through which the *psyche* —the physically conditioned *creature soul*—of the unconscious medium performs its operations. During the séance, the medium's psyche is subjected to a kind of hypnosis by the unseen, physical intelligences which manifest themselves in the reconstituted phantom shape.

That such a phantom wraith can even speak —indeed, will sound exactly like its dead and buried former occupant—is no more surprising than the ability to speak of any normally embodied individual; given that, for the duration of its brief appearance, the phantom body, too, possesses each and every organ that once had physically existed in its deceased original, including even bodily deformities and similar defects.

I trust there is no special need to emphasize that such a phantom shape, preserved in the invisible domain of nature, has nothing more in common with the human individual that once had been attached to it, than does a reptile with the slough it leaves behind.

୫

THERE IS a reason for my dealing here in some detail with facts whose very mention I find utterly repugnant.

I want to see you able objectively to judge phenomena that otherwise might startle and confuse you.

You should not let yourself be duped, for simple lack of knowledge, by things that only seem astounding.

To be sure, the fraud you may encounter in séances does not pose any real threat.

Serious danger is met only in authentic contact with these hidden beings.

୫

MY WARNING here is prompted by informed concern.

For if you ever should experience the effects these beings can produce, they well might sense in you another victim.

All too often do they find their prey among those seekers who, instead of striving to unite their timeless soul and find their God, will search instead for occult powers, without possessing the maturity and insight one must have before a Mediator—a fellow mortal who is conscious in the Spirit—is able to prepare them, in many years of strictest discipline, to master these demonic creatures and their frightening powers.

But even then there will be constant danger for anyone who needlessly attracts and uses them; and none who had to learn to subjugate this unseen realm of physical reality, in order to establish his authority, will ever stay there any longer than absolute necessity demands, in order that he may accomplish a specific task.

CHAPTER TEN

THE SECRET TEMPLE

ALL THOSE WHO HAVE BEGUN ALREADY to pursue the inner path ascending to the Spirit that I outline in this book, and likewise all who shall in future enter it, will thereby find themselves connected very closely in their inner life, even if a thousand miles were separating them on earth.

Such inner contact is established in two ways. First, by means of the reciprocal attraction of rays of energy, which self-directed centers of human will bring forth, without intent or knowing, in the form of radiant vortices in certain spheres of the invisible part of nature, where they connect all energies of equal kind.

Second, directly through the influence exerted by the energies that form the human soul, whose aims of will need merely to be pointed in the same direction in order to be linked at once with one another, and that without respect to space and time.

It is, however, part of human nature that those who feel connected by an inner bond, because they share a common goal, should want to know and be in touch with one another also in their life of physical experience.

Many also sense their faith and courage strengthened on their journey if they can sometimes share their feelings with like-minded seekers and companions.

And there are even stronger reasons why companionship and personal contact are often quite desirable.

The path ascending to the Spirit's life will oftentimes unfold more easily if those who have begun their journey become companions also in their outer life, and thus can travel side by side.

All who have been granted power and authority to offer guidance in these matters must therefore repeat the words of the sublime Master of Nazareth:

"Where two or three are gathered in my name, I shall myself be with them."

The Secret Temple

YET THERE must never be a larger group than two or three who come together to discuss and share their insights and experiences.

There are good reasons why so small a number is demanded.

Any larger group of souls connected by an inner bond can function in a beneficial manner only if that body is so structured that all discussions on experiences of its members' inner life remain confined to cells of two or three, of which there may be any number. Each of these cells, however, must be rooted in a feeling of the closest inner kinship of its members, so that its indestructible integrity is guaranteed from the beginning, even without special "vows."

Those who seek the Spirit's light should never form themselves into a "congregation," because no congregation can exist without enforcement of beliefs; and there is nothing less conducive to the soul's unfolding than all external pressure to "believe."

Congregations of whatever kind are nothing more than funeral processions of their members' perished faith.

As long as faith is still alive and active, it even may a certain time endure the gnawing ill that is a "congregation." But in the end, faith will succumb and die, like a flower blighted by disease, and those who thought they could assure its life by forming it into a congregation, will in effect have only dug its grave.

Many will, however, greatly benefit if they can share with one another things which they encounter or behold along their way into the Spirit, whether such a group remains alone or is in contact with like-minded gatherings of twos or threes.

Whenever possible, such groups of two or three companions should try to meet at always the same hour in order to exchange their inner knowledge.

Nor is there any reason in the Spirit's worlds which possibly might justify forbidding that any number of such groups of two or three maintain external contact with each other, provided only that such contact will not lead to forming congregations, which must demand belief in dogmas and in creeds.

Only then would such external bond destroy their inner unity.

The Secret Temple

BUT WHETHER you prefer to make your way alone or at the side of one or two companions, you always should remember that there exists a secret Temple, uniting you with all the others who have, like yourself, begun their inner journey.

The Luminaries of eternal Light are the appointed *priesthood* of this Temple, and every soul that seeks its inner way is safely guided by their help; even if it still were lacking its own light within, and could not yet distinguish its helper's guiding hand.

You here are not required to believe in help you cannot test.

The only thing we do demand of you is: faith in your own self, for lacking that you cannot reach your goal.

Once you have attained this faith within you, and continually reinforce it on your way, you soon will feel the truth of what I tell you—in your heart.

Those who found new continents beyond the seas had faith within their heart that they would find the lands they wanted to discover; and so they found what they had sought.

And in that way must also you have faith that you possess in you the energies that one day shall enable you in silent awe to witness in your soul the sacred mysteries and wonders of the Spirit's hidden Temple here on earth.

You need such faith in your own powers, because your faith alone can either set these powers free, or it will hold them bound and chained.

Whatever you do not believe you have the power to achieve, before you even try, you hardly will accomplish later.

So, too, will you remain beyond the reach of any help provided by that secret Temple until the day that finds within you the dynamic faith that you, indeed, possess the powers to attain that help.

# CHAPTER ELEVEN

KARMA

IN BOTH DOMAINS OF PHYSICAL REALITY—within the visible and the invisible dimensions—every deed engenders also corresponding visible, as well as physically invisible effects.

The concept "deed" must here be taken to include each impulse of your will, as well as every thought you think, and every word you speak.

You will remain encumbered by the consequences of your deeds until you shall have unified the energies that form your timeless soul and, using them, have been united with your Living God.

Not until that time shall you be able to undo the consequences of your deeds, to the extent that you would have them be undone.

ETERNITIES AGO you were united with your Living God, integrated as a purely spiritual being in the Spirit's all-embracing, all-pervading life and substance.

Your active will then also had the power to effect events throughout the vast domains that constitute the unseen part of nature—an immeasurable region of the universe—and you were the established ruler of these worlds.

The spheres in which your will had power to assert itself extended from the world of purest spiritual substance to realms of ever more increasing density.

And thus you came to reach the threshold where the spheres of the invisible become so much compacted that finally they turn to matter, and thus can be perceived by physically conditioned senses.

You saw eternal Chaos wield its terrifying might —the repercussions of the absolute, unmoving, spaceless Void—and you fell victim to their wrath against all things endowed with life and being.

But never would you have been fated to succumb to their hostility, had you not earlier, intoxicated with your boundless power, turned from, and so lost your God.

Karma

Thus, deprived of your sublimest might, you now were rendered helpless.

This caused you to fall victim to destructive forces, which are compelled to be forever active in the sphere in which the Void, the absolute, eternal Nothing, manifests its domination. And here, imbued with everlasting enmity, these forces struggle to annihilate—return to Nothing—whatever penetrates into their sphere: whatever *falls* from the domain of purest light into the darkness of their realm.

Even forces you had earlier been able to control, and with which you easily could have subdued the powers that were now your foes, so that they would have turned into obedient servants of your will: even they had now become too powerful, too great for you to master.

Thus, seized by terror of the very forces that had been your own and which you once controlled, you burned with longing for a new and different life; a life in the domain of physical, material nature—the universe that mortal senses apprehend—through which the terrifying forces of destruction are concealed to all who will not force their way into their sphere.

Your timeless will had fallen from the realm of highest light and now felt driven to escape with you into the world of matter.

You had your timeless home in the domain of primal causes, yet fear drove you away, out into the world of inescapable effects.

These are the actual events that lie behind the myths that tell about a "paradise" and of the human being's "fall" from grace in punishment for "sin."

✿

Before that fall, however, you had already shaped your karma, as Eastern wisdom calls the chain of consequences binding every mortal's fate: by the relative degree of your abandonment of God—the measure of your hubris—which caused you to regard yourself as being "God."

"You will be like gods, knowing good and evil...."

The age in which you would be born on earth, your ancestry and heritage as well as your specific lot in earthly life: all that you brought upon yourself when, having lost your Living God and, thus, dominion in the Spirit's realm, you were enslaved by powers of a nether sphere. Thus, you found yourself in a world where every deed

Karma

is linked to an effect, and must be so—because that world itself is merely a reflection of effects and, therefore, lacks the power of its own free will to terminate the causal chain.

Also, that your birth occurred upon this planet resulted from the nature of your primal deed in the domain of inescapable causality; for truly, there exist innumerable planets throughout the boundless universe which are inhabited by beings that are "human" and in effect resemble humankind on earth; and thus you might have found your creature body also on some other planet.

All those human beings who now inhabit planets in some other solar system had once experienced the abysmal fall from light, like you.

Among your distant, physically embodied fellow humans there are some whose lot is happier than yours by far, while that of others is much worse.

To be sure, you must not picture them in monstrous shapes; because the human being's earthly body on this planet did not evolve by some blind chance, nor only on our puny, solar satellite. It is, instead, determined by specific laws that regulate events throughout the universe of matter and ultimately have their origin within the realm of Spirit.

※

THE HUMAN being's fall from the domain of radiant spiritual life into the sphere subjected to the forces of eternal Nothing must not be thought of as a mythical event that happened only once and at a time beyond recall. Instead, it is a process taking place continuously throughout all eternity; just as this material universe in its unending cycles of creating and dissolving remains itself eternal as a whole, together with the Spirit's everlasting realm; namely, as the latter's outermost reaction and effect.

And always shall there be a few among the human beings born within the Spirit who do not succumb to that abysmal fall from light and, thus, remain united in themselves with God.

I spoke of them above as being the Elders, the Fathers of the Luminaries, who mediate eternal Light. And here I have to tell you, although you well might have deduced this on your own, that the enduring spiritual labor and concern of those who did not fall, as well as of their chosen Sons and Brothers, is not by any means confined to saving and redeeming merely humans that have

Karma

fallen from the Spirit's light and find themselves enmeshed in life, as mortal creatures, on our present earth.

Instead, the spiritual helpers of all humankind, who never lost their conscious life in the dimension of the Spirit, are found on every earth inhabited by humans throughout the infinite expanse of the material universe. And for each of all these planets they prepare their spiritual Sons and Brothers, whom they choose among the fallen spirits who are destined to be physically embodied on these worlds. And through these guides the Fathers also seek to reach *you* here and now, to lead you out of suffering.

By no means should you see it as your goal, however, to become one of their Sons and Brothers in this life, because for that it now would be too late; given that the faculty to reach this state reveals itself within a short time after the completed fall, and only through an impulse of an individual's free will. One then must gain experience, for thousands of years, during which one's incarnation in a mortal body is of necessity delayed.

The only thing here asked of you is that you will perceive—today, while you still live your life on earth—where you began your spiritual journey and whereto you once again are able to return.

One is prepared to show you the way back to your origin.

One seeks to guide you back to your eternal Living God, with whom you shall once more become united.

⁂

Although your fall has brought you very low, the energies from which the Godhead, without ceasing, forms Itself—rising from their lowermost, chaotic state to their sublimest self-expression —are nonetheless at work within you even now, and in a very high condition of their nature.

There also still abides in you—secretly and to your mental consciousness as yet unknown—a pure scintilla of your spiritual self-awareness: manifest within you as the guide that leads these energies and—as your conscience.

You cannot ever lose this spiritual scintilla in yourself, no matter to what moral depths you still might sink in life on earth.

Karma

Even if your consciousness is dead to its existence, it still must secretly abide in you until your final breath.

Nor is there anyone besides this radiant scintilla of the Spirit that knows the secrets of your karma.

※

You can improve the nature of your karma, and you can make it worse; only you cannot extinguish it before you shall have unified within yourself the countless wills that now still manifest themselves chaotically within you.

Once all these wills unite themselves within the radiant light of spiritual self-awareness, which is the true and everlasting human spirit in your individuated self, then shall your Living God be born in you, out of the Spirit's timeless substance, and then you shall at last be liberated from your karma—the causal chain that binds you to your primal deed—and you shall be a human self that has returned anew to life eternal in the Spirit.

Count yourself among the blessed if you are able to achieve this goal while you still live this life on earth.

If you do not succeed, then you shall likewise not experience inner peace even after you have laid aside your mortal form, until the day when you have found that peace within your God, conscious of your soul's united faculties, and now become their single, all-embracing will.

However, in that other life it may be ages before you can attain that goal; for then you can no longer influence, no more improve your karma; and thus you shall most surely not perceive the Spirit's light within you until the very last of consequences generated by your primal deed has run its course and been exhausted.

※

INDIA'S ANCIENT wisdom warns mortal human beings not to create new forms of karma, and such a warning clearly is the fruit of true discernment.

You ought to bear in mind, however, that this admonition is intended to protect you only from creating *evil* karma.

For in the Spirit's realm of living light you cannot find your ultimate "redemption," your "deliverance," until the last this-worldly, earth-directed impulse that once originated in your will has finally consumed itself.

Seek, then, with all your energies and strength to reunite yourself with your eternal Living God while you still live this life on earth; for thus you may, by virtue of God's power, cut the fetters of your karma, which otherwise might hold you bound for aeons in the life to come.

༄

CHAPTER TWELVE

WAR AND PEACE

Anyone who has observed the form-creating elements at work within the realm of physical perception, and who has grasped the terrifying powers, the indescribable simplicity of their inexorable drives, shall soon be rid of the illusion claiming that the universe we apprehend through our senses is but the visible expression of the Spirit's timeless harmony.

Consider only the ichneumon wasp, which is compelled to lay its eggs into a living caterpillar, so that the hatching larvae may sustain their life by causing their defenseless host to die in agony, and you shall be forever cured of that romantic fallacy.

The world we apprehend through our senses is the effect of primal spiritual energy, manifested in the Spirit's realm.

To emanate, however, as a spiritual world—within the realm of spiritual perception—the one, eternal, primal energy of Spirit must reflect itself in infinitely varied aspects of its essence. And once reflected in this manner, as an element imbued with primal Being, the Spirit's energy will now assert itself in every single element of primal Being with the effect that each of them must strive to manifest itself alone, and so will treat all other elements of primal Being as merely empty forms; for each knows only its own self as a reflection of the Spirit's primal energy.

Each aspect of the Spirit's primal energy—each element of primal Being—thus becomes the cause which then in turn engenders, also in its corresponding emanation in the realm of matter, the exclusive impulse to secure above all else that emanation's own existence and survival; a cause for which it will consume all other equally self-centered emanations.

Each element of primal Being embodies primal energy in undivided wholeness, whether it were to become the cause producing emanations of the highest or of the lowest kind in its respective realm.

And thus it is that every energy in nature, each physically perceived phenomenon, is striving to assert itself alone, as if no other than its own existence were intended to prevail.

The tiniest of cells is driven to sustain no being but its own, even if at times it is compelled, with billions of its kind, to serve a will creating higher forms. And to that will, the cell's existence matters only insofar as it is needed, and may be consumed, in order to assure that higher form's survival.

❧

THE UNIVERSE we apprehend through our physically conditioned senses is the utmost polar opposite of spiritual reality.

The Spirit's life itself conditions and engenders infinitely varied spiritual forms within its own dimension—the elements of primal Being—and their effect in turn conditions and engenders ultimately the domain we apprehend through our senses: the world of physical phenomena, whose forms appear immobilized and static; for here the Spirit's energy is "frozen" in a state of infinite "extendedness" and, therefore, relatively powerless; a state of being fettered by a rigidly-determined will that shapes the forms of matter.

Emerging from this state of fettered immobility and uttermost extendedness—a state completely alien to their nature—the Spirit's energies arise again, however, owing to the powerful attraction exerted by the realm where spiritual life attains its highest forms. And thus these energies find new, progressively less rigid and compacted forms, gaining freedom, step by step, and after countless transformations, from the tension generated by extendedness; until at last they feel themselves swept up into the Spirit's inmost life, where they regain the true condition of their origin.

What we, however, apprehend by means of our physically conditioned senses are not the elements of primal Being in themselves, in any of their given states, but merely the results effected by their power.

Nonetheless, within ourselves we can perceive the elements of primal Being on one of their sublimest levels; namely, as the elements that form our timeless soul.

Such is the unending, ever self-renewing cycle of eternal Life within the radiant substance of the Spirit, which is in Being through itself.

Self-consuming its own substance, the Spirit of Eternity descends to its profoundest depth: in order to arise again, receiving its own self into its highest form of being, completely free of immobility or form-inherent tension.

Only this eternal Life lets God create the Godhead in the Spirit—within the human spirit's timeless self.

※

BUT FOR THE blade of grass existing by the wayside, and for the webworm gnawing at its root, you, too, would not exist; nor would the Spirit's realm, or God within the Spirit.

But for the microbe which, perhaps tomorrow, may begin to break down your material body, your body, too, would not exist; nor would your soul, nor would the Spirit's radiant scintilla, whose life you harbor in yourself.

And then the Spirit's will itself would not exist: the will that once was formed as God within your timeless spirit, and now seeks to be born anew within your inmost self: as your eternal Living God.

※

YET ALL THE fury notwithstanding with which the elements may rage against each other in their struggle to assert their innate will throughout the universe of physical perception, nowhere in the realm of nature is there any hate.

It is foolish to see human hate in animals whose instinct drives them to kill other creatures; given that, like every form in which the elements of primal Being manifest themselves, they seek no more than to assert their own existence.

Hate, in reality, is an expression of mortal human helplessness.

Only by ascribing human feelings to them can one look upon expressions of aggressiveness observed in cornered animals as "hate"; nor is it difficult to see that those delude themselves who think they recognize in animals the same emotion which in human beings is defined as "hate."

It was by human beings that hate was carried even into the invisible dimensions of the universe; for their most dreadful other enemies within the unseen spheres of nature are equally incapable of feeling hate, and their hostility toward human beings has very different roots.

The most abhorrent fiends in nature's unseen realms are former human mortals who had doomed themselves by their own deeds on earth.

As high as they had once ascended in the Spirit's world, that far have they now fallen below the state of the most wretched mortal.

Eternities may come and pass before their life will be allowed to end at last, in nothing. But until then they seek to draw into their nether sphere whatever their relentless hatred can attract.

But even these invisible demonic beings, self-condemned by their own deeds, are driven to their ghastly hatred only by their sense of being ultimately powerless.

Yet power is the most majestic force to vanquish hate.

Those possessing power, being conscious of their might, love their sense of power; and thus may love in time inspire them in turn.

Love, however, brooks no hate.

The more the human race in its respective groupings, its peoples and nations, grows conscious of its Spirit-given power, the more will hatred vanish from the earth; for one who consciously possesses power feels no envy toward another's might; and envy all too often is the fiendish impulse that arouses hate.

All human wars have hatred as their father, and one who feels no hate is useless as a soldier.

Many voices nowadays still shout, "Make war on war!" They would be wiser to demand:

From now on let all hatred be rejected with contempt!

Not before all hatred has become contemptible will finally arrive the age when humanity shall learn to treat all warfare with contempt.

The day that any person is regarded as contemptible who would decide by mindless human slaughter what ought to be adjudged by rational discussions among the just and honest, only then may mortals on this earth be proud of their much vaunted "human dignity."

To be sure, there always will be conflicting views in human minds; for also here opposing wills compete with one another, and each is striving to assert itself alone.

However, in the human spirit, the individuated will can recognize its own self also in opposing wills. The human being, thus, is capable of seeking compromise, preserving peace through discipline of will, where then each individual will no longer shall be striving to assert itself alone, but likewise can assert the will shown by another.

※

But humankind shall not be able to pursue this path of discipline, of self-controlling will for long, until the day that each and everyone has rooted out all hatred felt within.

Consequently, war shall follow war, again and again, until the last and final trace of hatred shall no longer find a place in human hearts.

Whatever else may drive humanity to war can be surmounted by good will. The surging tides of hate, however, shall sweep away and drown the very best of human will.

Rivalry and competition between conflicting points of view develop energies of many kinds and thus will stimulate the very flow of life. But this need never lead to war; no more so than the winners in a game are forced to kill the adversaries they defeated.

All those on earth who strive to vanquish hatred in themselves are waging, thus, the only war one may call "just"—the war through which all wars of human slaughter shall one day become impossible.

※

Yet even when the human spirit shall at last have succeeded in banishing all wars of mass destruction from the earth, this cannot bring about that all the elements opposing one another, throughout the realm of nature, could ever unify themselves to be directed toward the selfsame goal; for such elimination of all conflict would mean the end of the entire physically experienced universe.

The realm of that "eternal peace" for which so many noble souls have longed throughout the ages shall be ours to enjoy, as human spirits, only after we have ended our mortal life; when we shall find ourselves once more in the eternal light that will forever reunite within itself what had been part of it in the beginning.

※

CHAPTER THIRTEEN

THE UNITY AMONG RELIGIONS

At the root of all religious teachings in this world one finds the same eternal truth, even if that truth is often draped in strange disguises.

Fruitless and irrelevant are all the arguments concerning which religious creed might still preserve eternal truth in purest form.

If one is able carefully to strip away all outer layers, one will discover at the heart of every true religion the same enlightened doctrine, telling us how once the human spirit had been one with God, but then had fallen from grace, because the human spirit in its timeless self had turned away from God.

The various religions then also show a path that leads the human spirit back, and ever higher, until at last it once more can be reunited with its God, within that spirit's inmost self.

But since this doctrine is by nature far too spiritual, indeed, too simple to be understood by humans on this earth as it was given, blinded as they are by the worship of things physical and complicated, which are experienced through the senses, they themselves concealed this final and profoundest truth, this guidance toward salvation, behind increasingly more curious veils; till finally the revelation of eternal truth had been so deeply buried under layers of conceited exegesis that one no longer could detect it beneath so many shrouds.

To be sure, the human soul still senses dimly that behind all that pretentious drapery and strutting pomp the truth had once been visible. And, thus, the mortal mind persists in clinging stubbornly to every shred of fabric once employed to veil the truth, which in the end entirely obscured it. This willful stubbornness of mind, however, believers call their "faith."

※

IN NOT A FEW of the enlightened teachings of ancient religions one comes across repeatedly, in one form or another, veiled accounts that speak of certain human beings in the Spirit's realm who never fell from the domain of light into the sphere of darkness, and who in some way influence

The Unity Among Religions

events on earth: as helpers of their fallen fellow souls confined in darkness, whom they would free again from being chained to earthly life as mortal human creatures.

Ancient legends found in such religions also tell us that these spiritual helpers of their fellow human mortals even had, from time to time, appeared in visible form; or how they chose their "messengers" among the "righteous" of the earth, who then were to bring light to all those in their time and place who lived in fear and darkness.

Often there is mention of a "sanctuary" high upon a mountain, or of a "mountain of salvation," or of "holy mountains" from which the world is said to be receiving help.

But while these revealing testimonies and many others like them can be found throughout the sacred scriptures of all ancient faiths, today one has no longer any grasp of what those words were meant to say. One regards them as mere allegories or, at best, sees their meaning as symbolic. Thus, misinterpretation has transformed what had been plain and lucid into self-invented error.

Yet the wisdom found in all religions of the ancient world originally had no other source than the instruction given human beings by their eternal Brothers, who still abide within the Spirit's world of light.

Their Sons and Brothers in the Spirit—those who have been incarnated in mortal human form and chosen to this end—sought in former times to give expression to the same eternal truth in many different forms, in order to bring light to human beings of all cultures, to each according to its kind.

All these revelations were sustained by the eternal Brothers' energy and help.

Here, then, is uncovered the one eternal source from which all ancient, true religions flow.

But where in our time are these religions' guides and teachers who really understand the meaning of the ancient texts they preach?

༄

YET EVEN as in ancient days, the timeless helpers from the Spirit—our elder Brothers, who had not known the Fall—are present also now on earth, in forms of radiant spiritual substance; and just as in most ancient times, they even now initiate into the Spirit's ultimate reality and truth whomever they find willing, directly following his fall from light, to become one of their future Sons and Brothers in this world of visible reality.

Humans on this earth have fallen far too great a distance from eternal light to make them still accessible to the sublimest helpers from the Spirit without the help of intermediaries.

And so these helpers will prepare the human spirits destined to become their Mediators, after being born on earth, embodied in a mortal form.

In and through these Mediators, then, the Spirit's highest helpers send their light and guidance, so that humankind on earth might never lack their helping hand.

Never has there been an age that lacked the help and guidance of these physically embodied Brothers.

They came to live among all nations of the earth.

Readers who have "ears to hear" may well perceive enlightened words from every age and time; words that "flesh and blood" could never have revealed.

Whoever would experience truth should listen to such words.

They will shed light on many secrets, and lift the veil that still conceals the final wisdom from the seeker's eyes.

ONE NEED not be endowed with penetrating intellect to note the difference between the pseudo-prophets in the streets, who make much noise, yet do not have a thing to say and, on the other hand, the Brotherhood of Luminaries who offer help in silence.

Wherever on the ruins of some ancient shrine there rises what is merely a new sect, even though it proudly call itself a new "religion," one never should assume the Mediators of eternal Light could have a hand in such associations.

One would be closer to the truth if one suspected that the lords of the abyss, who reign in the invisible domain of matter, the serfs and vassals of the Prince of Darkness, inspired such new sects; even though there is much preaching about "love," and many pious phrases fill the air.

What those who mediate eternal light are giving you will surely not be in the form of yet another "new religion" today, when you can barely save yourselves from religions and everything you label with that word.

And yet, it is the same eternal truth that rests within the core of all the ancient, true religions.

Here, one merely shall reveal to you that core anew, without its veils; showing you, in new,

The Unity Among Religions

transparent images, adapted to the present age and to the future, realities which, in the garment of religion, have long since lost their meaning in your life. And thus you may with true respect approach again what all the great religions of the world preserve within their heart.

Eternal truth as such, without all veils, cannot be shown you by another; not even by a Luminary in the Spirit's light.

That truth you must unveil alone, within yourself, in silence.

For in yourself alone can the sublimest of all wonders manifest itself as absolute Reality.

Only in your own eternal self can you regain, one day, what you had lost before your mortal life on earth.

※

YOU ARE NOT just the short-lived mortal creatures of this earth—animals endowed with higher reason and intelligence—as you may judge yourselves according to your physical descent and history.

Not only higher, but also far profounder things are hidden in your nature.

When you say "I," you just assume, by force of habit, that this word denotes your real self.

But to this day you do not know what *self* embraces, in reality, within yourself; for conscious *self* is infinite and can be actively experienced on countless levels of awakened life.

Each of these levels will, through all eternity, perceive above itself another, still higher level of experience.

And each perceives beneath itself innumerable lower ones, like steps descending to the limits of the deep.

Your life today, however, is more like that of animals, which have no conscious self within them; although your world is steeped in art and science, and your existence all but sated with material pleasure.

When you shall one day have awakened in the Spirit, you cannot but with horror look back on the way you live today, without concern or care, as if such frivolous existence realized the highest forms of life to which your kind could ever hope to rise.

CHAPTER FOURTEEN

THE WILL TO FIND ETERNAL LIGHT

I know there will be not a few among the readers of this book who find the world it puts before them unacceptable, because it is in conflict with their own view of reality, which they deduced with penetrating intellect, or stubbornly believe to be the truth, so that they angrily reject what here has chanced to cross their path.

Needless to say, their hostile attitude will scarcely force reality to modify its given structure, which must remain the way it is, and always was, and ever shall be.

Let no reader be deceived!

These pages were not written by a troubled mind attempting to describe ecstatic dreams.

Nor by a poet seeking to depict his visions.

What is provided here is guidance one can trust; for every word is founded on reality.

Those who until now have not been able to discover this reality may learn to understand it; and the path to such an understanding, which in itself embraces and utterly surpasses any other form of knowing, is shown them in what follows.

Every reader will be well advised, however, to bear in mind from the beginning, that the very elements of spiritual being, illuminated in this book from many different perspectives, are ultimate realities. Realities by far more real than anything considered "real" in the common usage of the word. And, furthermore, that these realities continuously manifest their power, even if the human being is still ignorant of their existence, or willfully refuses to acknowledge their effect.

This will doubtless have some consequences for many who now learn of all these things. Yet they shall only benefit themselves if they begin to recognize reality as such and, thus, can doubt no longer that their former "worldview" was rather an illusion; notwithstanding that it looked to them completely true—because they trusted physical appearance—and even if the mirror-like reflections of their mind already seemed enlightened from within.

The Will to Find Eternal Light

STANDING STILL is to regress, according to a proverb. In fact, however, standing still is worse; for even going back can lead to valuable insights, which shall not be attained by those who are too lazy or too stubborn to abandon their "position" for the sake of seeking truth.

Yet those who are afraid of ever turning back, have at the same time every reason to distrust advancing.

There is no progress without limit here on earth.

All humanity's development is subject to the laws of alternating rise and fall.

Humans today have lost much knowledge and ability that, to their distant forebears, seemed established for all time. And where these forebears had but little knowledge and ability, humanity today has reached astounding insights and capacity.

The one thing nature will not brook is idly standing still.

"Would that you were hot or cold! But since you are lukewarm, and neither hot nor cold, I will spit you out of my mouth."

This is how eternal law has spoken throughout time, and to this day it has not changed its words.

❦

Those who tarry in spiritual darkness are still not willing to experience light.

They well may *wish* to see the light of which they hear others speak, but they themselves still lack the *will* to find it.

As soon as it in truth becomes their will, they shall have also found the way that leads them to the Spirit's light.

If you believe the Spirit's light is worth devoting all your strength and energies, you truly shall one day be able to approach that light.

As long, however, as your inner eye is covered by a heavy veil, it is not possible that you could *see*.

Your will alone—not your most ardent wish—can lift that cover from your eyes.

If you assert the will to find eternal light within you, then you shall indeed attain that light; whether you approach it slowly and with caution, or as one whose heart and soul are burning with desire.

The Will to Find Eternal Light

But you will never reach your goal if your resolve is fickle and half-hearted.

There is no other God in all the universe, and not beyond the farthest stars, whom you might reach and move with your pathetic pleas.

You must resolve to help yourself, if you would have your Living God—whom you can only find within you—support you with high help, according to the cosmic laws that have their source in God.

※

Your timeless self embraces all reality that is in Being, and every phantom that deludes you is of your own creation, as you unknowingly misuse the energies inherent in your self.

Before your life on earth you caused your separation from the Godhead, when you no longer would know God within your timeless being, because you sought yourself where only God abided.

Thus did God for you become a separate being, and you to God a stranger.

And now your mind envisions a divided self, imagining a "higher" and a "lower" kind embodied in your nature, because you do not know the true dimensions of your undivided self, which is but one and cannot be divided.

And so, there is no "higher" and no "lower" self existing in your nature. But in your one and undivided self lies hidden all infinity, and it embraces the sublimest heights and the profoundest depths in the dimension of the Spirit.

You alone will have to choose what is to be revealed within your timeless self; and here your choice is solely manifested by your deeds.

In your own infinity—within the center of all Being that your self embraces—will then once more be born your Living God.

Even then you will at first experience God as different from your own being, until at last you recognize that all your undivided, timeless self is now embraced by God.

CHAPTER FIFTEEN

THE HUMAN BEING'S HIGHER FACULTIES OF KNOWING

YOU BELIEVE IN YOUR IDEA OF "PROGRESS," but do not recognize that you are moving in a circle.

Restlessly you labor to dissect, dissolve, and analyze whatever you encounter, and as it cannot be denied that you have gained considerable knowledge in this way, you feel convinced that this pursuit must one day also lead to the solution of all remaining mysteries of physically experienced nature.

But everything that has been split and sundered can be split again, potentially *ad infinitum*; and time and again it will be found that things one had believed dismantled to their ultimate components will nonetheless reveal still smaller particles.

The limits of all scientific probing are determined only by the physical impossibility of splitting and dividing things beyond a certain point.

The incapacity of going any further, thus, defines the last results of scientific searching.

I certainly appreciate the debt that humans owe to this form of inquiry, and far be it from me to slight the way of thinking it demands.

But I see also the defects of that approach, and how the mortal mind allows itself to be deluded by its own discoveries, so that the human being becomes continuously more detached from a quite different, but in the end far more important, kind of searching.

By virtue of your method you have already found astounding things, inventing much that truly is amazing.

However, that should not mislead you overconfidently to embrace the view that in this way you also one day might gain knowledge in domains that shall through all eternity defy mechanical analysis; dimensions that no instrument can measure, nor detect.

Having once discovered the smallest elements that constitute a physically existing structure, the human mind is doubtless capable of drawing

The Human Being's Higher Faculties of Knowing

practical conclusions, based on given laws of nature, and thus resulting in developments which in the end may prove of great significance for our life on earth.

The inmost essence of the structures thus unraveled, however, remains as enigmatic to the human mind as it had been before.

To be sure, your work and the results it has achieved deserve profound respect and admiration. Nonetheless, the "thing-in-itself" will always lie beyond your mental grasp; even if you knew each object in this visible creation down to its smallest particles and understood each atom's marvelous configuration; even if you knew how each and every particle behaves and could manipulate its energies at will.

The "thing-in-itself" will never be detected under any microscope, nor shall the greatest of observatories shed any light on what is holding distant galaxies together.

ଔ

THE INNER drive to know and to explore is an integral part of human nature and this desire must be satisfied.

But you entrusted all the work of searching only to the creature senses of your nature, while letting the sublime potential of your soul, whose faculties could here advance your purpose, lie dormant in the twilight of your consciousness without developing their powers.

And so the creature side within the human being equips itself with vehicles facilitating mental operations, and with enormous instruments, in order to extend its thought and probing to infinity. But all results it thus obtains lead only to still further questions, in face of which the mortal mind at last no longer finds an answer.

In ancient times, however, there were human beings who looked upon this method of pursuing knowledge as mere folly; mortals who, by virtue of their soul's sublimest energies, which they had integrated in themselves, were capable of solving the profoundest mysteries of being—without the modern world's gigantic apparatus.

They found the way that leads one to the ground of Being, while modern thought enlarges but the surface.

Full of learning you can say of everything in nature why it appears the way it is perceived; why things will function under some conditions, while under others they will fail; and countless details of that kind. Still, for all your knowledge, you are not getting any closer to the final causes;

given that, whatever you consider *causes* are nothing but *effects*, behind whose workings only reign the final causes; and these transcend the mortal mind's experience.

But once your inmost self has learned to master the energies that form your timeless soul the way they must be ruled, these energies will clearly show you even the profoundest causes; for they are one with them in essence, although they differ in the form they manifest themselves.

To be sure, one cannot offer proof to demonstrate these causes, except to those who have themselves already learned to use their soul's inherent energies. Scientific proof, by contrast, is easier to offer, although here too one first must have acquired the prerequisites for understanding the basis of such proof.

※

No FACULTY can be developed unless it is used.

If, thus, you fail to use your soul's inherent energies in even little things at first, they never shall grow strong enough to show you their most wondrous powers.

Much remains to be discovered here that truly would be worth the efforts of a lifetime, even if one were to live a hundred years.

But first you must become simple in your nature, even as the final things themselves are simple, if ever the least complicated mystery of all is to reveal itself within you.

Your thinking has become far too complex, so that today you can no longer grasp reality in its profoundest essence without first learning how to think in a quite different way.

A common experience accessible to everyone may here provide an illustration.

For much was not so long ago considered rampant superstition, until your own research revealed to you that this apparent false belief was based upon a valid insight, which you had merely failed to see, while minds of very simple nature were able to perceive it.

All readers here will have enough examples of their own, so that I need not mention any in particular.

There likewise still is much concealed in legends, myths, and popular beliefs, and even in some outright superstitions of the common people, which future generations may come to see as fruits of tested knowledge.

The Human Being's Higher Faculties of Knowing

The reason that these things are still not recognized today by those who seek to find them in a different direction, with the help of science, may be found in the incredible complexity of our day-to-day, routinely practiced way of thinking. The mortal mind rejects employing simple concepts because it is no longer capable of using them, unless it first forgets the greater part of what it learned in school, even at the lowest level.

A great deal, thus, appears all but impenetrable to external probing, and only with painstaking effort is a little of it brought to light.

But nothing of this knowledge can be hidden from the energies that form the human soul, if they are once sufficiently developed.

It is for you, the present generation, to determine whether your descendants shall, in days to come, be forced to bow to realities that you today could have uncovered, or whether you instead bequeath them knowledge they can trust.

ଔ

ALSO EVERY revelation of eternal truth that now lies buried in mythology and folk belief had once originated in the insights gained by mortals who had learned to use their soul's dynamic energies.

Regrettably, the inner darkness that benighted their successors prevented these from comprehending what they had received; and so the pristine truth was quickly overgrown by weeds of idle speculation, and now can scarcely be distinguished behind that thriving growth.

But those who search with confidence and patience in their soul will there detect the same eternal well of knowledge from which the ancient sages once had drawn their wisdom. And then shall they in fullest clarity possess within themselves what now is barely recognizable beneath the overgrowth of false beliefs, but then shall become lucid—by virtue of their own experience.

However, without patient seeking in yourselves, pursued with no less dedication and resolve than you today devote to searching in the world outside, you never will experience what the energies that lie concealed within your soul are able to effect.

You are vessels holding wondrous powers, while in your outer life you labor for a pittance.

The higher faculties of knowing to which I here would draw attention reside in every human being; yet they lie dormant in a leaden sleep, until their owners shall awaken and unite them with their own inherent will.

The Human Being's Higher Faculties of Knowing

Most mortals end their days on earth without so much as having sensed the very faintest glimmer of the timeless treasures they had harbored in their soul.

Blest, indeed, are all those who can awaken their higher faculties of knowing while there still is time.

For they shall find their true, eternal life already here on earth, and discover their immortal selves in even this dimension of mortality.

❦

AND THAT IS, after all, the prime intent behind all spiritual instruction. For what imaginable purpose would be served to speak of spiritual existence—which we possess through all eternity—if this existence were so far beyond the grasp of mortal humans' own experience that they could never even hope to reach it during life on earth?

Only what we have experienced here on earth can also guide and help us understand our life to come, the day when we shall have to leave this physical dimension.

❦

CHAPTER SIXTEEN

ON DEATH

HERE WE FACE THE DREADED GATE through which all mortals have to pass when they depart this life on earth forever.

You were promised great rewards, but also threatened with grim punishments that are supposedly awaiting you beyond.

I do not know which of these teachings you believe are true.

Compelled by everyday experience, however, all will agree on at least one point; namely, that you never can return to this life in your present mortal body once you have finally left it.

༄

SOME WILL TELL you that you shall indeed return, but in a new material body and at some future time. And to this end they have devised ingenious rules that are to govern your return to earth within another mortal form.

Others deem that, with the dissolution of your mortal body, the rest of you shall likewise be destroyed forever; for they believe no more than what they see, and when a person dies they only see a lifeless form, revealing nothing that might lead them to conclude that the departed could still in some way be alive.

In fact, however, both opinions are mistaken.

To be sure, it is unlikely that you will yourself return to earth, but no one knows how many of your soul's dynamic elements you will be able to retain, as being integrated with your timeless self, the day you leave this earthly life.

All those elements not unified within your self you then must leave behind, the same way that you lose your mortal body. And even as your body's elements, whose recent, time-restricted form is now dissolving, are undergoing changes to seek other forms of life, so also shall the elements that used to form your soul, but which you failed to integrate within your timeless self, now strive for new means to express themselves within another human being.

In your own soul, too, are active many energies that had already been at work in other human lives, before your time on earth.

Indeed, one justly could distinguish human mortals by the age of their respective souls as being *younger* or *older*, depending on the length of time their soul's dynamic energies already had been active here before, in human beings of an earlier age.

In a generation of human beings born the same year, there are many in whose soul are found much younger elements than are at work in the majority of their contemporaries, and likewise not a few with elements that are considerably older.

One may recognize the like exceptional cases even in their daily life, in that such persons' sensibilities will often differ sharply from the way that other people of their time, indeed of their own generation, are known to think and feel. They are not, as it were, in step with their own time, but rather with the spirit of an age just past, or even one belonging to a very distant time and culture. This need not, to be sure, prevent such persons from being well attuned to life in their own day; in fact, they often will contribute works of lasting value to their age.

THE TOTAL number of the energies that constitute your soul at any given moment is continuously changing all your life, as long as you inhabit your material body.

At times there will be more, at other times you will find fewer of the energies that manifest themselves within your soul.

Furthermore, if death should separate you from a person for whom your soul felt deep affection, you scarcely will sustain that loss without "inheriting" some of the energies that formed that person's soul; for very rare, indeed, are mortals who can retain, and take with them into their life beyond, every single element at work within their soul on earth, unified in their eternal self, and thus united with their Living God.

The majority of human beings leave behind them a most plentiful inheritance when they depart this present life.

Eyes that see within the Spirit's world perceive your soul as a dynamic, luminescent cloud, containing countless radiant *sparks*, which are the elements that form your individuated soul. And this dynamic cloud of light is subject to continuous change and motion as long as you shall live on earth.

On Death

The actual riches of your soul, however, are not determined by the enormous wealth of all the energies that are at work within you, but rather by the sum of only those that you were able to unite within your self: within your timeless will, which is begotten of the Spirit.

The only elements within your soul you will retain, and thus possess for all eternity, are those you shall have integrated with your timeless self the day you bid farewell to life on earth.

※

IF YOU WERE not united with your Living God while you still lived on earth, then you shall likewise not be one with God the day you leave your mortal form.

You then will live within the all-embracing Spirit as a conscious self, in your own form of spiritual substance. The nature and potential of that form for your continued self-expression will then depend on the degree of spiritual development you had attained in life on earth.

You will continue on your inner journey, guided by the Spirit's helping hands, until one day your Living God is born within you.

The time until that day, however, will appear to you as an eternity; for also in the Spirit's life, freed of the material body, there are equivalents of what on earth we know as time and space.

But you will then no longer have the power to increase in any way, and by your will, the scope and number of your soul's remaining energies, which henceforth shall provide your only source of what you will experience in the Spirit.

You now must be content for all eternity with no more than those energies that you were able to unite within your soul while you still lived on earth.

Even so, however, no human self will ever feel the slightest longing to return to life on earth, no matter what it had to leave behind, no matter how impoverished, how destitute of energies its soul might enter life in the domain of Spirit, where then it will continue and complete its way to God.

※

A SECOND life on earth, though in a different form, is nonetheless a possibility, but only in three special situations.

First, in the case of those who must endure it in consequence of the great evil they committed in their life.

On Death

Secondly, for those who would not let their mortal organism live out its appointed time, depriving it of self-experience, in the belief that its destruction might allow them to escape a seemingly unbearable degree of pain or other forms of anguish.

And, finally, for those whose time on earth had been too short, so that they had no possibility of unifying any of their soul's dynamic elements in their eternal will. If they were not afforded a second chance to integrate the needed elements —and this can only be accomplished during life on earth—they would eternally remain incapable of knowing life within the Spirit.

That also is the reason behind the other two exceptions. In the former instance, one is dealing with a human self that proved incapable of unifying any of its soul's dynamic energies, even though its life span would have been sufficient, because the animal-directed instincts in the person's nature had suffocated the required higher will. In the other case, the individual had forfeited whatever energies it had already integrated in its soul; namely, at the instant when the person's mind succumbed to the obsession of having to destroy its mortal body, the organism given it on earth that it might thereby manifest its timeless self.

※

THE READERS for whose guidance I here provide these explanations need merely bear in mind that nothing but their own misdeeds can burden them with having to endure, a second time, the suffering imposed on life incarnate in a mortal body, constantly subjected to every force and influence of this material world.

Yet if human spirits who, by harsh necessity of nature, were deprived all too early in life of their material body—the organism needed to express their timeless self—can thus attain this instrument a second time; indeed, if physical conditions should again have interfered, even several times—then this is doubtless a provision that all who now begin to sense how crucial is this life on earth for the return of fallen human spirits to their origin, can only fathom with profoundest gratitude: as a necessary consequence of that sublimest Love which in itself embraces all creations of the Spirit, even beings that have fallen very low.

May the readers of these words retain them in their hearts, and come to recognize with ever

On Death

greater clarity that their existence here on earth endows them with the awesome power to decide the nature of their future fate themselves.

The proper way that power should be used is clearly set forth in this book.

Yet no reader need be apprehensive about the fate of those departed from this earth who had not in their mortal life attained the level of development at which their Living God could be born within them: where, with the energies united in their inmost self, they could become united with their God.

For, truly, everlasting Love embraces also them!

All those that ever found their Living God within themselves are then their most devoted helpers; for in the radiant substance of the Spirit's realm all energies at work in human souls are linked with one another. And whatever those who are already one with God had once attained on earth, and what they now experience in the Spirit, in this way is communicated also to those human spirits in whose eternal self their Living God is not yet born.

This help is at the same time guided by the sublime immortals who never knew the Fall from

God, and who are leading back into eternal Light —both in the world of Spirit as even here on earth—any fallen human self whose will is to return to the condition of its origin.

See that you make every effort to attain your highest goal already here on earth, but fear not for the souls of those who were unable to accomplish it in their own day.

You can, however, also offer them your help if you remember them with feelings of abiding love.

They all shall one day be united with your own eternal self: within their Living God.

One with God shall you then, in yourself, be consciously united with all those whom your own love can embrace.

CHAPTER SEVENTEEN

ON THE SPIRIT'S RADIANT SUBSTANCE

THE WORLD IN WHICH YOU LIVE ASSOCIATES the concept "spirit" with attributes of mood and mind.

"Spirit" in the language of that world denotes the faculty of thought and forming concepts; it also may connote a person's disposition, or the real meaning, true intention of a thing.

As for the Spirit of Eternity, however, whose radiant substance is a real, objectively existing force illuminating all creation, it sees in all the faculties which are today ascribed to "spirit" merely tools of physical—all too material—perception.

Your present world has knowledge only of the Spirit's tools, and owning them believes it thereby also comprehends the Spirit in itself. And, thus, your soul's all-seeing "eye" was blinded by the "spirit of the world."

Now that this "spirit" dominates and leads you where it will, you shall no longer easily resist it.

⁌

THE SPIRIT OF Eternity, which consciously exists in its own light, is not some nebulous mirage that only pious faith might fathom.

Eternal Spirit is not only quite as "real" as is a tree, a stone, a mountain, or as a bolt of lightning that flashes from a cloud, but its *reality* is absolute within itself. It thus provides the justifying grounds for our mental concept of "reality," which has no true equivalent in the contingent realm of matter.

But given that not even objects of contingent, physical reality are altered in their nature by any thoughts about them held in human minds, how can one seriously presume that mental notions might affect events of *absolute* reality?

The mental image of a thing reflected in your thought will never even touch the smallest object in the world of matter in its real essence. Nor can the Spirit of Eternity be comprehended by any-

On The Spirit's Radiant Substance

thing you may call "spirit" while you have not yet grasped its radiant substance in yourself.

༄

TODAY, AND at this moment, you well may think you sense the truth my words convey, but come tomorrow, you are likely once more spellbound by the "spirit of the world."

Today you may be willing to escape it, to seek the Spirit of Eternity, but I fear that by tomorrow you will again be blinded by the "spirit" of the mind.

Today perhaps you feel that you have sensed a glimmer of the Spirit's radiant light, but tomorrow you will likely be beset again by doubts and indecision, and thus give up the effort to pursue what you this day felt almost within reach.

That is what your kind has always done when someone spoke to you about the Spirit of Eternity, whose radiant light embraces all creation; someone who had leave to speak about that Spirit, because he lived in it awake and, therefore, could bear witness to its essence from personal experience.

Perhaps, however, there truly are a few among you determined to exert all energies, so that they may one day themselves experience the reality of which I speak in its ineffably majestic, uttermost simplicity.

To them I shall address myself, for they alone can profit from my words.

༄

To you, then, who resolved to give the "spirit" of the mind no more in future than its due, lest it rob you of experiencing the Spirit's radiant substance in yourselves—to you I here repeat once more that you may etch it in your hearts:

Spirit is not something brought forth by the mind!

Spirit is not intellect!

Spirit is a radiant substance: is living light, eternally in being through itself!

All dimensions of infinity are filled with this life-giving Spirit, whose light sustains all living things; but human beings can find that Spirit only *in themselves*.

It consciously exists and lives in you, even as it consciously informs all spheres throughout creation.

It is not only in your *head*, nor merely in your *heart*.

The human being's mortal body may be animal in nature, yet this same animal-related organism mysteriously encloses and conceals a body formed of Spirit.

Truly, you are *temples* of the Spirit, and every limb and inner organ of your mortal form contains within a sacred shrine, placed upon a hidden altar.

Therefore, you must first have learned to feel your *self*, from head to foot, through your entire body; for otherwise you cannot ever *feel* the Spirit, nor consciously unite yourself with your eternal Living God.

This kind of feeling of your self through your entire body, which conceals within a sanctuary of the Spirit, must become your foremost task. And everything I said before already comprehends this task, even though I spoke of it in different words.

Here I shall discuss it in particular.

∞

You must endeavor to attain a consciousness that is not merely in your heart, nor only in your head.

Consciousness abides in you and it pervades your body through and through, informing each and every cell. However, it is not yet integrated with your present conscious self.

But if you are in earnest and will be steadfast in your efforts, you will be able to discover, step by step, in every part of your material body, its own inherent consciousness. And this you then may so unite with your own self-awareness, that henceforth you no longer only know a little of yourself within your head, and even there, more accurately, only in your brain.

Do not excite, nor over-stimulate your nerves, however; for this way of becoming conscious of your entire body is something all of you already know too well.

If your soul does not grow calmer, nor sense more clarity with every step that you advance, you are pursuing the wrong path.

If you would reach your goal, you must endeavor, while your soul and body, nerves and thoughts are perfectly at peace, to feel your *self* in every atom of your body—where you are soul by nature—as that atom's very *soul*. You thus may integrate within yourself the primal energy of soul that, in and through that atom, you possess.

On The Spirit's Radiant Substance

You need not here perform mysterious "exercises," nor are extreme exertions called for or of any use.

Calmly feeling your own *self* through your entire body, whenever inclination moves you and you have time to concentrate on this experience free from interruptions, will show you, in the course of weeks or months, the first results of your endeavor.

Do not forget, however, that your task is learning how to feel exclusively your self in every limb and organ of your body, but not that body part as such.

Once you shall be able in this way to feel your *self* both from within and from without, from head to foot, you will experience with amazement, with gratitude and deepest joy, what life on earth consists of in reality; this mortal life which now still seems to you so flawed with imperfections.

At the same time, however, your entire body will be undergoing a wholly unexpected and profound renewal.

Those who lack some of their body's limbs should bear in mind that every limb is in existence in its spiritual form and substance, even if it never had existed physically; and similarly, that every limb continues to exist in spiritual form, even if it should be severed from its body.

The *body* formed of spiritual substance can never be disfigured.

In their spiritual body, all human beings manifest the highest form of beauty with which they can endow their soul: wherein their spiritual body gains its self-experience. And those whose eyes can see within the Spirit's worlds perceive of any body only what has found its form by virtue of the soul's dynamic energies; they do not see defects of merely physical appearance, resulting from the intervention of material forces.

※

When you have reached this point, where you can feel your *self* as one organic whole through every part of your material body, then you shall truly also know to treat that body with due reverence; namely, as the visible, material form of the eternal *temple* which encloses, hidden from all physical perception, the sacred mystery of spiritual life, such as it may be regained and experienced only by the human spirit returning to the Light which long ago that spirit had abandoned.

It still needs to be seen, however, whether the awakened soul already is mature enough to let

On The Spirit's Radiant Substance

the spiritually older Brother, by whom it is perceived, become its guide and teacher.

Without such inner guidance none of you would have much hope of gaining consciousness within the all-embracing Spirit already during life on earth, even though you may be able consciously to feel your *spiritual body*, present in your mortal form.

No effort that you make is ever lost, but to receive your labors' crown you first will have to reach the end of that ascending path which no one finds without the help of inner guidance.

Much, however, you are able to accomplish on your own, merely by consistent effort.

The moment you have learned to feel your spiritual form throughout your mortal body, you will begin to *breathe* the Spirit in yourself and all creation, without especial effort; and to many this alone had brought such joy that for a long time after they felt no desire to go further, because they sensed they were not ready to experience higher things.

Fear not, however, to accept whatever you are given and trust the Spirit's law, which is not governed by capricious will, but always seeks your best.

The path that leads you to the Inner East lies clearly marked before your eyes, and your awakened will alone shall now determine whether one may soon observe you on that path.

The realms within the Inner East, however, encompass "many mansions," and all who seek in earnest shall there obtain their own abode, never that of any other.

The laws that govern spiritual events are no less well defined than those which rule in nature.

The Spirit's laws cannot be set aside or modified, not even by a Luminary, who mediates eternal Light.

He understands the workings of the Spirit's laws, however, and thus he seeks above all else to guide his own contemporaries, as well as future generations, to their highest goal and joy.

To this end he offers his disclosures.

Herein he is supported by the Spirit's law, whose will he serves with all his strength.

What he effects is done by virtue of the Spirit —the essence underlying the Beginning—and he works nothing save by virtue of the Spirit.

On The Spirit's Radiant Substance

But from the Spirit's radiant substance God creates the *Living God*—as the quintessence of the Spirit—in every human soul that strives toward God with fervent inner zeal, and patiently awaits the day that finds it so prepared that it can bear the birth of God within it.

God, indeed, is Spirit—the highest form in which the Spirit manifests Itself.

Forming its own essence, of itself, the Spirit's highest form of Being reveals its inmost self as—God.

CHAPTER EIGHTEEN

THE PATH TOWARD PERFECTION

WHEN SEEKING YOUR GOAL IN EARNEST, be sure to choose the path of living light already from the start, as otherwise you later might be easily seduced to enter the deceptive path descending toward the "iridescent serpent," when you have reached the foothills of the sacred mountains—a place that one perchance may also reach on furtive byways—instead of following the path created through the desert by the Spirit's guides.

You can decide to take that path of living light from the beginning, if you will keep all lesser aspirations from your great and pure resolve.

But would you still possess the inner strength to choose the royal path of wisdom, which is to lead you to the snow-capped peaks, if overburdened with desires you trod your way across the desert and, near exhaustion, you now are searching for the final goal, only to encounter soaring walls of rock?

Bear in mind that to your soul the light of truth shall then appear as no more than a distant glimmer through the mist, and that the path ascending to that light will seem as all but endless.

Yet winding nearby is the path of error, which leads one to a gleaming, opalescent light appearing almost within reach.

That light, however, is the phantom luminescence of the "serpent," whose body's coils encircle all the earth, glittering in many colors.

Your fate is sealed if you succumb to its allure.

It will attract you by the ceaseless glitter of its scaly head, and once your thirst for "knowledge" has drawn you far enough into its sphere, you shall become that serpent's prey.

※

CAN YOU, my friend, intuitively grasp the truth that here would reach your understanding in symbolic guise?

Count it as a blessing if you can learn to comprehend what symbols truly mean.

They shall reveal to you profound realities.

Realities that otherwise would as a rule remain concealed.

Realities that never would display themselves unveiled.

Here I shall attempt, however, to speak to those as well who still find symbols enigmatic.

Listen, then, to different words, but bear in mind that they convey the selfsame truth.

☙

WHEN YOU, whose will is seeking light, shall for the first time feel the urge to raise the veil behind which you can sense the truth, there will always stand beside you one among the guides from that domain of light which shall become your timeless home.

You will be conscious of that helper's presence without quite knowing what it is that moves your heart.

You will feel drawn spontaneously to follow where your guide shall lead.

You then are truly on the path that takes you through the desert.

That desert is created, however, by the countless grains of mental sand which mortal minds produce in gathering external phantom knowledge.

For millennia have humans labored to expand it.

But through the middle of that desert runs a solid causeway, raised by ancient builders, who are masters of the craft; and here your step will be secure.

Drifting all around that highroad move the ever-changing dunes of mortal intellection, elusive in their outlines; unsteady ground to tread.

The path, however, on the causeway, which the Spirit's radiant masters built for human souls, is raised on ageless rock.

You feel safe as you proceed.

Your stride is marked by courage.

Patiently you will have to pursue your goal for quite some time, until you one day reach the crucial point where finally the causeway through the desert's sands will meet the sacred mountains, where it thus will end.

And now you must decide; because you see two paths before you, which you at first may not be able clearly to distinguish.

At times you will be drawn to put your trust in one, and then again you feel inclined to trust the other.

One, however, leads you to the summit, the other to the groundless depths and hidden gorges in the mountains.

You alone have now the choice and must decide which path you want to follow.

You will not find it difficult, however, to tell which path shall lead you to the heights and which to the abyss, if you already are accustomed to feeling solid ground beneath your feet; for slippery and without foothold is the path descending to the realm below.

Already on your way across the desert, which you traverse on solid rock, invisible realities shall seek to make their presence known to you.

But then you cannot yet distinguish the originators of the forces whose effects you will perceive.

You still assume all energies originating in the sphere of the invisible are governed by the self-same will.

Bear in mind, however, that the nether realms of the invisible domains are ruled by beings that are likewise from below.

Recognize that land and sea are not so clearly set apart as are the lower forces which, creating and destroying, invisibly sustain the world of matter, from the timeless powers of the Spirit, whose way of knowing truth embodies light itself.

The forces ruling in the lower spheres of the invisible domain are the most gruesome enemies of your eternal soul.

Not because they want to harm your soul, as would the hate-consumed obsession of those fiends—condemned eternally to perish—who once were human mortals endowed with highest knowledge, but who had fallen from the realm of light a second time; instead, their danger to you lies completely in their power of attracting you—a force you hardly would be able to resist, unless you are securely shielded by protectors from the Spirit.

At times when you come near domains affected by the influence of forces from below, it will become apparent who you are.

If what you seek is purely timeless clarity and light, your inner guide, who, after all, has power

The Path Toward Perfection

to direct the Spirit's highest forces, will be able to protect and shield you.

Under such protection you then will safely know to choose the path that is to lead you to the highest form of comprehending light.

You then will enter life within the timeless light that shines upon the Spirit's radiant peaks.

But if your aim was only to acquire knowledge in the crude "black arts"; if you intended merely to explore the sphere of the occult to gain new faculties to wait on your desires, then you will unknowingly lose hold of your protector's hand.

Thus left alone, dependent on your own weak strength, you will fall prey to forces of attraction, whose influence upon you is directed from the nether sphere of nature's hidden rulers, where in the dark of the abyss they govern the eternal birth of matter.

You may—perhaps—gain occult powers, especially if you abstain from meat and practice strictest sexual abstinence; but pity both yourself and all those falling victim to your influence if ever you indeed gain power of that sort.

THOSE WHO rule within creation's nether spheres are weaving nature's very ground, and they destroy whatever would be free to rise above the ground they labor to secure.

Do not delude yourself assuming they could teach you any secrets of creation, as some foolish "sorcerer's apprentice" might naively hope.

Instead, they greedily shall take possession of your will; for every power found in the invisible dimension of reality requires *human mediators* if it seeks to reach and influence incarnate human wills. You, however, shall only serve these nether forces as an agent of destruction, even if you think your actions are inherently constructive.

In fact, the highest powers in the world of Spirit can reach the souls of human mortals with their influence no more easily than can the lowest forces in the unseen realm, unless they find incarnate human wills to serve them as a bridge.

You here may sense the meaning of the doctrine teaching that the Son of God needed to be born in mortal form that he could bring salvation to all humankind.

The Path Toward Perfection

THE WORKING ways of spiritual powers, whether their effects be generated, and their character determined, by the highest or the lowest rulers in the unseen realm, are not affected by any obstacles of time or space.

To this day there are in action, in the domain of human souls, forces generated and determined both by powers from above and from below, even though these forces had already found their way to human hearts many centuries, indeed millennia ago—by virtue of a human bridge.

Wherever such a Mediator lives on earth today, or may have lived before, the spiritual energy made manifest through him will reach all human souls of corresponding inner *rhythm*, even if those able to perceive it were living on the planet's other side, or were yet unborn, being members of a future generation.

True guidance to the Spirit's world is easily distinguished by the fact that every energy it activates will always carefully respect the inner freedom of the person in whom it manifests itself. Indeed, such guidance typically perfects the mortal serving as its bridge, to make him sovereign master of the energies he mediates. By contrast, one can tell the rulers of the lower spheres by their attempts to bind the persons they can influence, through everything they may affect, so that those persons will become their slaves; even though they let their victims think that they are "masters" of the forces that possess them.

The end of one who serves these lower rulers as their bridge is dissolution of the conscious self in agony and night.

Those, on the other hand, who serve the Spirit's highest powers as their bridge comprise an everlasting royal priesthood of eternal light; for within each was lit a star, formed of the Spirit's purest radiance, that is to shine forever to human souls on earth.

An idle, fabricated doctrine would persuade you to believe that human mortals rise to ever higher levels of perfection in the course of countless earthly lives, and that the bridges who build themselves so that the Spirit's highest powers may, through them, reach humanity on earth, are simply human beings who had already lived on earth innumerable times before, but now have reached their highest level of development; a goal, supposedly, that one day every mortal soul is destined to achieve.

The Path Toward Perfection

Do not believe such foolish dreams.

For you might all too easily become a victim of deception, and suppose that you shall be a "future master" but instead end up a slave, betrayed by your own vanity.

※

NOT EVERY mortal can take up the burden which the few alone must bear who, soon after their own fall from light, and strengthened by compassion for their fallen fellow mortals, had pledged themselves to serve the Spirit's highest powers as their helpers—as bridges who will build themselves—in the fulfillment of eternal love.

No one here can pass his final test who had not been a bridge and master builder already in the Spirit, and long before his incarnation in a creature body here on earth.

As a mortal he will consciously become the Spirit's bridge and master builder only on that day when he may first approach the radiant circle of his spiritual Brothers, as one who also in this physical dimension had proved himself a master, having passed his final test.

Who until then had been a Son of the eternal Fathers in the Spirit has now become accepted as their spiritual Brother, is made a Luminary of eternal Light.

※

But every mortal human on this earth, whoever it might be, is able to attain and manifest the Spirit's light, in freedom without end, even if that mortal will receive that light as does a planet orbiting a sun.

In the worlds of timeless light no spirit looks with envy on another's working sphere, bestowed upon it by the One who is the Master of all Masters' craft.

All who have attained this realm have reached perfection, are free within themselves, and all are quite aware that their perfection could never have been realized except *in their own individual form*.

It only is your limited perspective as a mortal creature that might cause you to desire a form of spiritual perfection that is not demanded by *your own* eternal individuality.

What would you gain by reaching a perfection whose form must needs belong to someone else?

The Path Toward Perfection

Even if you had attained perfection of the highest form that mortals may achieve on earth, and if this form were not *your own*, you would have labored to no purpose to achieve this goal.

Only if you shall perfect what *you alone* are given and possess; only by perfecting *your own self* will you one day attain that everlasting light that shall illuminate your soul forever.

CHAPTER NINETEEN

ON EVERLASTING LIFE

I HERE SHALL SPEAK OF LIVING LIGHT: THE everlasting Life that nothing can destroy in all eternity and which imbues all Being that is human.

I want to make you see the light that shines within your heart, which lives in you and can illuminate your being.

All of you that sought the meaning of this mortal life have far too long already followed ways that only lead to error.

You now shall find what you were seeking, if you will trust the words of someone who has found.

You are like royalty who live in ignorance of their own realm.

In yourselves alone you find the timeless realm your eyes shall seek in vain as long as you expect to see it in the world outside.

⁂

ALL YOUR questions go unanswered, but you continue asking, "Where is the kingdom we were promised?"

"Shall our being simply disappear the day we leave this present life, or shall our consciousness survive when our mortal life has ended?"

Comprehend that those who in their day had asked the selfsame questions are alive within you, present in your inner realm, and that they here could answer what you ask if you had not grown deaf from all the noise in your external world.

Your own eternal soul is, finally, the *kingdom of the spirits* who shall live within and with you through eternity.

Within your timeless self you comprehend Infinity.

Within you lives what is, what was, and what is yet to be.

On Everlasting Life

Your very self is timeless presence within all dimensions, but you are still confined to being present only here and now, within the physical domain, where you keep waiting for events that never come.

You still believe the kingdom of eternal peace is far away, a realm beyond the stars, while in reality that kingdom lives within you, and you yourself are living in it even now.

※

WHOEVER HAS attained that kingdom within becomes its sovereign forever.

As you shall there encounter human life of every kind in its eternal essence, so too, shall *you* be found within that realm: in all the others who possess it in themselves.

It is a single realm encompassing all spirits, but each among the countless souls who found this realm within will own it undiminished. Each one becomes its sole, unchallenged sovereign whose reign shall last forever; as if, indeed, no other ruled this inner realm, which all among the multitudes rule also as the kingdom of their own soul alone.

You cannot find the Spirits' realm outside of your own selves.

For only *in yourselves* can you indeed attain it.

Your searching in the world outside would needs subject you to illusions; for everything outside the timeless world of your own inmost self is no more than a fleeting *image*—experience enduring but a little while—as is this life on earth, which is cut short by death.

Where the eternal soul abides within itself, integrated with and guided by a conscious *self*, there at last we find the kingdom that shall never end.

There alone one is secure from all illusions.

Only there eternity becomes our very own.

It is your timeless self that is alone the all-possessing sovereign of this eternal realm.

※

The sovereigns within this timeless realm are infinite in number, and all who gained that kingdom as their own become united in themselves with all the others who rightfully here wear their crown; for each remains the one and only sovereign, through whom all others rule.

On Everlasting Life

All those that here have found eternal life dwell with and within one another; not separated or apart.

Just as here on earth one says that people "live their life" when actively they use it to some end, be that good or evil, so likewise in the Spirit's realm to *live* means to be *active*. Life implies activity and is not merely a state of being.

"Life" here is the light that shines within the conscious human spirit: the very light by which that spirit lives.

You are yourselves entwined within the timeless world of spirits, and through your being flows all everlasting spirits' life, but you are not aware of it.

In what you call your "self," which you at present only sense as a mirror-like reflection imparted by a reflex of the brain, you think you are distinct and isolated individuals.

Everything imbued with Life, however, is constantly united with *all* living forms.

Neither here on earth, nor anywhere within the universe, and nowhere in the Spirit's world could anything have Life, could anything exist in isolation, merely on its own.

Every individuated form of being is, ultimately, all of Being.

Even if that being lacks the faculty of comprehending that reality.

The individuated being can attain *salvation*—liberation—only when it shall experience its existence as a part united with All-Being, freed from every other form of separated life.

You thus will find *salvation* only if you learn to sense in your own *self*—within the timeless *self* which shall be yours forever—that all the other *selves* will only give themselves to you in this, your own eternal self: united with themselves for all eternity.

Within the self in you that is eternal you embody all of Life, and only in that Life you find the beings who, in truth, are called *eternal*, because their life is without end.

You might have found them long ago if prejudice and stubbornness had not misguided you to seek them only where they never shall be found.

In vain you try to force your way into the unseen realms within the world of matter.

More easily, indeed, could one of the Eternals appear before you in broad daylight, in visible,

On Everlasting Life

material form, than that you might encounter him in nature's hidden realms.

You must descend into the depths of that which in your own self is eternal if you would consciously unite yourself with those who have already entered everlasting Life.

༺

CHAPTER TWENTY

THE SPIRIT'S LIGHT DWELLS IN THE EAST

F︎EW IN THE WESTERN WORLD TODAY DIVINE the truth when they hear about the "Wise Men of the East," whom high-minded seekers after truth in esoteric circles know from old traditions; and few of those who dimly sense what is implied are able to resist exotic fantasies when they attempt to give their intuition concrete form.

The East, the heart of Asia, holds the lands where human mortals most sharply honed the razor-edge of intellect.

But here, many thousands of years ago, had also lived the great lights of the Spirit who, far above all mental thought, had found the lucid path to truth: the truth which is Reality and, therefore, differs fundamentally from all the speculative images of knowledge that commonly are deemed to represent what one considers "truth."

They were the first among the Brotherhood of Mediators here on earth, and they pursued their path and goal protected by the Spirit's highest guidance.

And ever since have they and their successors offered guidance, from the Spirit's realm and by the Spirit's power, to any human soul that is prepared to benefit from their instruction.

They raised a sacred wall of silence around the presence of their Brotherhood, and only those will find acceptance in their midst whose spirit they will judge mature enough to be endowed with knowledge of the Spirit's world.

They know that only those can profit from their gift who are already near their journey's goal, where all the trials of their path shall end.

To all humanity, however, they are sending guides and helpers from their midst, as they have done throughout the ages.

Both in Western and in Eastern lands there always have been members of that Brotherhood whose work required living in the world.

The members of that timeless spiritual body are not identified by any outward signs.

They alone are able to distinguish who is of their kind.

Their spiritual essence and identity remain concealed to mortal eyes.

※

NONE OF THE Spirit's helpers to whom I here refer will ever seek to found a congregation around his person in this life.

None of them has ever instituted any such community of followers.

Wherever "congregations" of that kind originated in the world and claimed to have been founded by the spiritual Brotherhood, if not indeed its radiant Fathers, such groups were always organized by only partially developed souls, who, owing to their prematurely active inner senses, had been able, like eavesdroppers, to catch fragmented insights from the circle of the Inner East. They were not, however, able to interpret properly what they had overheard.

Only seldom has a member of that Brotherhood explicitly professed his spiritual identity before the people of his time, so much preoccupied with temporal affairs, and for each who took this step such confidence became a bitter sacrifice.

Unless that kind of sacrifice is absolutely necessary, it is thought better to avoid it.

That is why the Wise Men of the East provide their help without revealing who they are.

That is also why each member of that circle keeps his background to himself, unless he is compelled by his specific mission to disclose, either in symbolic terms or more directly, the truth about his spiritual identity, which is a heavy burden to acknowledge.

~

THE SPIRITUAL Brotherhood of Luminaries—age-old traditions among devoted seekers after wisdom know them as the Wise Men of the East—is governed only by the Spirit's law.

Its members take no vows to live ascetic lives, nor are they bound by pledges of religious or secular orders. The development of spiritual powers does not depend upon such things.

However, what is called for by the Spirit's law, which these powers will alone obey, is more severe by far than even the most rigorous asceticism and the harshest life of penance.

One must abandon many preconceptions whose premises may in themselves be valid, but which pertain to no more than the lower energies, if one would know what makes a spiritual initiate who is admitted to that circle.

You, however, will be known by any member of that body, even though your concepts of his nature might be wrong.

Nor will his teaching be through words your ears are able to perceive.

The words that one who is united with the Spirit may speak or write in his own language do not comprise his teaching in the truest sense.

Such words are only meant as *hints* to help you find again both him and others of his kind within you—within your inmost self.

Yet also words he speaks or writes are meant to be absorbed and felt; not analyzed, nor intellectually dissected.

If you are able to become his *pupil*, however, his voice will "speak" to you within your heart.

He never shall becloud your mind and senses with ecstatic raptures, but shall instead unfold within you new and *spiritual senses*, in addition to your body's faculties.

Initially you will perceive his "voice" without quite knowing whether what you "hear" might be the friend and teacher of your soul, or rather your own self.

A new, specific feeling of great purity, which is imparted by his words, will soon reveal to you, however, that what you hear within is spoken by a sacred voice: a voice creating inner clarity directly, without the medium of human speech.

This often unexpected, spontaneous experience of receiving inner clarity on matters of the Spirit —a clarity immeasurably surpassing the enlightenment we commonly attain through reasoning and logic—will always offer you a certain sign that what you are perceiving is authentic inner guidance.

A teacher in the realm of Spirit is not seeking to "convince," but rather sheds immediate light on what had until then been hidden in the dark.

In this way a human *brother* speaks in you who has no longer need of sound waves, air, and mortal ears if he would have his teachings reach receptive hearts that trust his guidance.

The Spirit's Light Dwells in the East

AT FIRST you may perhaps not fully understand what you experience in this manner; for one can certainly perceive events in perfect clarity, yet be unable mentally to analyze what has been witnessed.

Be calm and patient in that case and do not cloud what had been clear by idle speculations.

Above all else, learn clearly to distinguish the voice in which your teacher "speaks" in you from the deceptive "voices" of your excitable imagination.

Maintain objective self-control and quiet, as if you were observing long-familiar things within you.

At the beginning of his guidance your teacher's voice will seem as faint as an elusive thought, an almost imperceptible emotion.

The inner guide, however, does not speak a single word in his spiritual language from which does not emanate a readily distinguishable feeling of true certainty, which is not easy to describe, but will be recognized immediately by anyone who felt it even once.

No thought of one's own mind, even were it of the most lofty kind, can ever bring about the feeling that is brought forth by the Spirit, the source from which the inner teacher speaks and by whose power he performs his work.

The more your certainty increases in distinguishing his voice from everything that is not of his kind, the more distinctly can he speak in you.

And so you once shall see the day when even your most hidden doubts will have forever vanished from your mind.

※

Yet do not grow impatient if you cannot all at once attain the first among your inner goals.

You have no way of knowing whether you already are mature enough to benefit from being taught, and here it is your teacher who alone must bear responsibility for everything he gives you.

For some the day of final knowledge will come sooner, for others it comes later; it will assuredly come, however, if you entrust yourselves in patient confidence to him who guides you from the Spirit.

Also bear in mind that real wisdom is objective knowledge of *reality*, and that authentic teachers of such wisdom base their teaching on only *that reality*, which is certainly not the most complex phenomenon in all creation but, on the contrary, the very essence of simplicity.

The human mind is prey to forces that always covet to deceive, because they only live by practicing deception.

The guide who teaches from the realm of Spirit is far from their domain.

Nor shall what he conveys to you at any time concern things other than realities of Spirit, of the soul, and of eternity.

Through him you shall discover your eternal *self* and also what the human being in its essence does ultimately represent—in truth— within the cosmic order.

Trusting him who guides you in yourself, you shall attain the same degree of inner certainty that he himself possesses.

His own eternal certainty shall he that has found certain knowledge now also grant to you.

You should not ask him questions in yourself, however, before you have experienced the great hour that is to bring you final certainty.

For if you do, you surely will fall prey to those deceptive forces of the mind.

Nor should you try to form a picture of the mortal nature and appearance that your teacher in the Spirit might possess on earth; and if you know of one who lives in union with the Spirit, you must not all too readily assume that he will be *your* inner guide.

You do not have to know which one among the Luminaries, who mediate eternal Light, might be your inner teacher; and those who know shall never tell you.

Keep control of your imagination; for else you might be led with open eyes to wander after phantoms.

The earthly life of one who teaches from the realm of Spirit is his concern alone, and he would not have anyone mistake the Spirit manifest in him for that which merely is his temporal appearance here on earth.

He does not want his pupils to bestow the honor that is only due the Spirit to the mortal person through whom the Spirit's power works.

He teaches no more than the *wisdom* one calls *truth*, and which reveals itself within the pupil as absolute reality.

He teaches wisdom only in the Spirit and through the Spirit's power.

Still, anyone who has authority to offer inner guidance in this way will always be most painfully aware that any imperfection in representing absolute reality is but the work of mortals; and every Mediator of eternal Light shall take any honor shown his earthly personality and sacrifice it forthwith upon the timeless altar he was called to serve as an appointed priest.

CHAPTER TWENTY-ONE

FAITH, TALISMANS, AND IMAGES OF GOD

SIMPLE, AS THE VERY GROUND OF BEING, are nature's final mysteries.

Let not your thoughts' capricious will draw lines dividing things that owe their being to a common root, and you will everywhere observe the workings of the selfsame laws.

But you were taught to build yourself another world, a world without foundation and cause; and this construction, in your mind, of a non-existing world from nothing, your teachers called your "faith."

This is not the "faith" I mean when I here use that word.

You do not need this kind of "faith" to gain your soul's *salvation*.

Instead, we want to make you conscious in yourself of an eternal *energy* that is alive in you and which, forever active in dynamic motion, unceasingly creative, collects the forces of your will and gives them form to be effective.

※

FAITH IS creative energy within the Spirit.

Faith creates the inner form through which your will can manifest its power.

Faith is the creative form through which your will becomes effective.

You cannot truly manifest your will unless you draw on faith; for will that has no form is energy diffused and, thus, is spent without effect.

As soon, however, as your will is given proper form, by virtue of your faith, it shall become a power strong enough to alter even the apparently unalterable chain of physical events, so that its iron links shall melt like wax, to take the form determined by your faith.

Your soul is starving while you live devoid of faith, and in its need it even will seduce you to believe in superstitions.

Faith, Talismans, and Images of God

Will is the very life of your eternal soul, and every kind of *will* would find the firmly anchored form through which it can effectively express itself.

When you begin to feel what *faith* embodies in reality, then you truly will be able to employ its power.

※

YOUR FAITH provides the "mold" in which the liquid metal of your fate is given concrete form.

Your faith needs total freedom.

You are yourself your faith's unique and only norm.

Your faith shall form your God in your own image, even as it once had formed your idols.

Divine reality in its unfathomed depth is ever without form.

You, however, can only comprehend its ground when it reveals itself as manifested form.

To you it shall reveal itself in no form other than your own eternal self.

Thus, you cannot show your God to others for they cannot behold your God in all eternity.

Others see the same eternal Godhead, but formed in only their own image.

You still assume you can sway others to make your God their own, but if they thus allow themselves to be misled they would pay homage merely to an *image*, and in this way their own God would to them become a stranger.

Endless are the forms in which the all-embracing One is revealed as timeless Being, and heaven help all those who would dispute even one of all these myriad shapes.

The selfsame instant that you shamelessly unveil to anyone the inner image of your God, that very instant God is lost to you.

Do not imagine that, in all the multitudes exalting God in a particular name, you could find even two devout believers who worship the same Godhead in that name.

※

THE ENERGY of faith itself, however, can function through the name of any god or devil.

The creative inner force at work in faith, which gives direction to your will, constitutes the single cause of all effects attributed to "magic."

Faith, Talismans, and Images of God

All magic power, "white" or "black," is rooted in the selfsame force.

Even as the elemental power which in nature manifests itself as lightning can be bound and stored in metals and containers—a force that can be put to use when harnessed and controlled—so can the energy of will that has been formed by faith be bound within material objects.

In all religious cults, among all nations, you will encounter human faith in certain holy objects, believed to be endowed with sacred powers.

You scoff at such belief and call it "superstition."

If here you only have in mind the fables that have overgrown such objects like a clinging vine, then you may not be in error; however, guard against disdaining the reality concealed behind such things.

୰

Any object you imbued with will, its power well defined by faith, becomes indeed a "talisman." The virtue of such talismans you often have experienced, although you did not realize what rendered them effective, nor would have in your dreams suspected that you in fact surround yourself with "charms."

To be sure, the object in itself is but the *vessel* holding and preserving a dynamic force that is by nature free, but which has now been bound within that object.

The object does not of itself possess that inner force.

Your faith had formed the power of your will, and then conveyed it, as a rule without your knowing, to the vessel in which it is preserved until it shall be spent.

You continue to "recharge" that object with new faith, although you may not see it as a talisman.

Any object you employ in order to assure success in one endeavor or another, although that object is not, strictly speaking, needed for your task, is actually a talisman; even though, as an "enlightened" mind you would deride it as a superstition if you were told of people who employ such objects consciously, certain that they can rely on their effect.

Such people are aware of what they do, only you act without knowing.

૭૮

It is the same with any image representing God.

Faith, Talismans, and Images of God

Be it the fetish in the dwelling of the primitive, or the majestic statue of Athena.

Be it the painting of a saint revered within the towering cathedral, or the wonder-working triptych in the ancient cloister.

All these are *vessels*, holding the collected inner energies of countless people who had formed their will by faith and had been able to implant that will into the object of their worship. Even the pathetic physical remains, the relics of some holy person, whether genuine or spurious, may serve believers in that way.

The faith of those believing in these objects then becomes the key that will in turn release the energies contained in them.

Consequently, no one can release such powers who does not believe in them; for only faith creates the high degree of tension in the currents of your will that can impel the well-defined, accumulated energies of other wills to flow into your own and, thus united, function as you will.

※

We here do not suggest, however, that you make use of all the talismans of every cult.

Nor would we counsel you to make a trial of the faith-empowered energy implanted in the images of gods or holy saints. Nonetheless, you should not mock these things if you would truly comprehend the law at work behind their veneration.

The workings of that *law* is all you need to recognize, and what it offers you in life on earth you should endeavor to make useful for your purpose.

Your will is not at all times manifesting the same strength; but if you form repositories of your energies whenever you are strong, you shall experience nearly miracles at times when you feel weak.

Any object you like using, or which you find around you every day, can serve you as a vessel to retain and fortify the powers of your will; and when your strength at certain times is ebbing, you can release again the energies you need and which are held in the repositories you created.

Best suited for this purpose, however, are objects of great beauty.

Things that owe their very being to consummate mastery of form shall best preserve for you the energies that have been formed by you.

Faith, Talismans, and Images of God

Surround yourself with objects of that kind, which you can day by day imbue, at moments of your highest strength, with the specific energy you need whenever you feel weak.

Always have such objects with you, wherever you may go.

Believe that you are able to transmit your power to such objects, and that you likewise can withdraw it from them any time you wish.

Truly, such *belief* is not mere "superstition."

You still do not suspect how very "real" are the forces of your will, nor do you sense what powers you possess once you have learned to form your will by virtue of your faith.

Do not destroy your faith, however, by idly speculating how such things could be "explained" by present-day psychology.

If you hear someone talk of "autosuggestion," you must not let such terms confuse you.

Words like that can here provide no explanation.

One simply coins a novel term, but this will not account for an effect which rests upon sublime internal powers.

The realm of nature acts according to its innate laws; it does not wait for you to offer "explanations" justifying its activities.

What we know of these things I here have clearly shown you.

Whether we convey the truth, you can discover only if you put this knowledge to the test.

CHAPTER TWENTY-TWO

THE INNER FORCE IN WORDS

I<small>F YOU WOULD FIND WHAT YOU ARE SEEKING</small>, you need to know that every age requires its own kind of inner forces; you must not, therefore, be misled by doubts if you do not see evidence of the identical mysterious energies in every age.

Those having power to direct what here must be directed shall always guide the river's flow into the driest regions of the land.

In our time you should not, consequently, look for the effects of any inner forces except the hidden energy in words.

༄

A<small>MONG ALL</small> hidden energies, the *word* embodies the sublimest inner force.

A time will come when, simply by the word's inherent power, things shall be achieved on earth that verge on the miraculous.

Truly, "miracles" shall one day be performed by virtue of the *word*.

Miracles far more astounding than all the signs and wonders humans worshiped in the past.

There shall arrive an age when, by the word alone, one shall accomplish works that would today require countless hands and huge machines.

To be sure, that age is still a very long way in the future.

Humans today are not yet able effectively to *speak* the word.

But even in the darkness of the present age the word already is beginning to reveal its power; for humanity's path has reached the threshold of a brighter realm, whose promise offers hope and comfort also in the dead of night.

Observe the world around you, and everywhere you shall discover signs foreshadowing the inner force in words, sometimes even in distorted forms.

It thus becomes apparent that what the word is able to effect is more than just transmitting messages from mind to mind.

The Inner Force in Words

You would be wise to heed the witness of such signs.

※

BE EVER mindful of the word!

All your life you have been told that words as such had little value.

The only thing you were to search for was their meaning.

You thus became accustomed to seeking chiefly mental "understanding," and in this way you lost your heart's most precious gift, the last remaining spiritual sense you still possessed: the faculty of inwardly discerning things that you experience.

If you would see that inner faculty restored in you, prepare yourself not merely to consider words according to their meaning, but always seek as well to sense their very form and sound within you.

※

YOU SEE, IT is not simply chance, but the effect of cosmic law which causes words to be imbued with hidden power; so that the highest inner energy becomes embodied in the form and substance of the word. Consequently, there are words—words in languages of human mortals—that could dislodge a mountain if the force confined within them were set free.

There are words your understanding would be powerless to comprehend, and yet you cannot utter them without their inner force producing its effect upon your soul; even though you are by no means able to give them voice in such a way that all their energy would be released.

I could tell you wondrous things about such words, but you would not be able to believe me.

What will convince you is alone your own experience.

Bear in mind, my friend, that all things in creation possess their *rhythm* and their *number*.

Rhythm and *number* constitute the elements from which all inner force derives.

Those who can detect these two already hold the key that opens this mysterious gate.

What I discuss here is not meant for them.

There is, however, not much likelihood that any such will come across these words.

Few are those who have ever found that secret key, and those who did will only read one everlasting book: a book wherein each *word* is life, and every *sentence* signifies activity.

※

NOR AM I able to "explain" to you what rhythm and number represent within the universe.

I here mean only to instruct you to be mindful of the *word*, so that through words you may discover what in this age you would in vain expect to find in any other form.

Give proper heed to words, and you shall soon be able to distinguish truth and error in things pertaining to the Spirit.

All wisdom rooted in the Spirit approaches you in its own rhythm of eternity.

All things of ultimate reality are wearing cosmic numbers on their fillets when they appear in the garment of words.

Those are much mistaken who believe that the sublimest, deepest, and most secret wisdom of a sacred book—a book composed by one endowed with timeless knowledge—could be gathered from the meaning of its words.

Such meaning, doubtless, can shed light upon the depths of the eternal ground; all things of ultimate reality, however, and their profoundest mystery, your inner sense must fathom from the sound, the form, the very kind and value of the words themselves.

You must not think that even one of those who have mastered the ways of rhythm and number has ever been indifferent to how he placed his words.

Poets search above all for beauty; seers give their words eternal voice.

One may recognize the seer even when the seer is a poet; nor can the poet hide the seer when concealed behind poetic words.

❧

IF, THEN, you wish to learn how you can feel the life of words within you, any word found in your language may serve you as your teacher.

Yet do not search for "meaning" once you have decided to pursue this path in earnest.

"Meaning" cannot stay concealed for long; it is determined to be known.

Attempt, instead, to *hear* within yourself the words through which you seek to learn.

You will in time be hearing them as if it were another's voice, and this shall be your first true sign that you, indeed, are on the path of learning how to hear the sound of words that voice themselves; for truly, words possess the power to pronounce themselves.

The word of the eternal Spirit, too, *explains* itself, once you have learned to *hear* it in yourself.

Yet even if your intellect be razor-sharp, it must keep silent when the word itself is speaking.

You must allow the Spirit's word to come to life within you, so that it may reveal its deepest wisdom to your soul.

But do not think that here you merely play a game, which one enjoys a little while and, losing interest, will put aside.

If you would truly profit from this counsel, you need to practice every day with never failing patience, until the day arrives when finally the Word in all-pervading resonance will know itself within you.

Then only shall you truly grasp, by virtue of your own experience, what insights words are able to convey.

Many doors shall then unlock themselves, where now you knock in vain to have your questions answered.

Then also shall your mind more clearly understand the real sense of many a book that now seems full of riddles.

I shall not tell you more than you must know.

Begin your work with confidence in your success.

The times are favorable for this quest.

You will be gaining much by daring but a little, without too many questions.

But bear in mind: what you pursue is not a game for idle moments.

Only constant dedication shall crown your efforts with success.

CHAPTER TWENTY-THREE

A CALL FROM HIMAVAT

Throughout the world is manifest a deep desire, an all-consuming inner need, and every soul not yet completely hardened, no longer capable of growth, is moved by the experience of this longing.

Seas of human blood* have drowned the jaded skepticism which, not so long ago, had seemed a mark of intellectual sophistication.

Today, it is again acceptable to believe in things that cannot be made evident by scientific proof; nor is one any longer ridiculed for recognizing that invisible realities surround and influence our life on earth, even if we have not yet deciphered that dimension.

---

*A reference to World War I. The first and second editions of this book in the original German were published in 1919 and 1927, respectively.

Miraculous events want once again to become realities, and the domain of faith continues to expand its borders.

Souls that seemed but lifeless stones and dead to any impulse from the Spirit have suddenly awakened—in a hail of thundering blows unleashed by frenzied, rage-filled demons—and now are forcefully alive; even the great mass that lies in torpid sleep shows signs of growing restless.

With every dawn their spiritual awakening can be expected to draw closer.

Minds that have awakened, however, shall be demanding answers from those who kept them sleeping for so long; and with contempt they will reject all "teachers" seeking, with pretended piety, to limit any questions one might ask, given that they have no answers.

༄

Humanity has at last grown willing to perceive itself as belonging to this earth.

No longer will it dream of gods enthroned upon the clouds, and ever closer comes the day when —likely for the first time in its history—it will experience in itself the meaning of the words long since addressed to it by one who spoke with God's authority:

"The kingdom of heaven is at hand."

Those who claim to be the "servants" of the divine Anointed, however, saw fit to raise a towering wall: for the protection, they insist, of all the souls who, in the radiant Master's words, possessed the kingdom *in themselves*.

Individuals who never in their lives had found the inner kingdom here so clearly promised, usurped positions of authority to dominate the souls of their own fellow mortals; based on a belief in their possessing wonder-working faculties, a fiction used to justify mere lust for power and to quiet their own conscience.

They barred the gate of heaven to all others, as thoroughly as it was closed to them, and diligently rephrased every revelation of reality in such a way that what remained were merely verbal forms and symbols, well suited to inspire dreams about the kingdom of heaven; for they knew very well one did not need them to attain eternal life.

Only the naive could hope the prison wall they built to hold believers' souls in bondage would one day, surely, have to crumble before the rush of those attempting to escape.

Too strongly is that bulwark reinforced by the cement of mortal greed for power.

Also, there are not a few who want to always feel surrounded by that wall, and so one must not ever take it from them.

Too long accustomed to a life in bondage, they would but perish being free.

To be sure, the signs and symbols chosen to disguise that wall shall differ through the ages, lest those enclosed by it should recognize they are imprisoned. The wall itself, however, shall endure as long as human thirst for power can count on finding souls in fear of judgment and damnation; and on this mighty rampart, firmly joining threat and promise, anyone is doomed to perish who undertakes to breach it—from within or from without—before its time has come.

꼰

THERE IS A way, however, to escape that bulwark's tyranny without the need to breach it.

Souls whose time of waking up is near shall of themselves develop wings and soar above the sphere of mental spells cast by the very powers that gladly would prolong their night of sleep and dreaming.

A Call From Himavat

We see the day is not far off when many souls shall finally awaken.

The task allotted us is to direct the flight of those who have arisen to regain their freedom, and to guide them toward the sunlit peaks of the great mountains, the radiant snows of Himavat.

Still, there is need of many helpers; for the awakening that is to come will be experienced by great numbers.

We do not want a single soul to lose its way, to perish from exhaustion in some desert.

Yet we can give direction only to the gathered flock of all the newly liberated as a whole, and anyone resolved to help us should look for souls that went astray, lest, victimized by phantom goals, they lose all sight of their intended path forever.

Our call goes out to anyone who will support our work unselfishly.

All who in their hearts will pledge themselves to help us show the way to those who lost direction are able and invited to assist us.

The only kind of help required here is wise, compassionate support; no one, therefore, can become our helper who imposes help on others.

To offer help the proper way means guiding by example, so that the soul that went astray is able to regain direction on its own, without discussions and persuasion.

Perhaps your help is hardly noticed, yet each of you redeems a debt that you have owed for aeons, if but a single soul is led into the Spirit through your help.

Let those keep far away, however, who offer their assistance with great fanfare, seeking to promote themselves in merit and importance over others.

Nor have we any use for busy and officious meddlers.

No one can here lend a helping hand who is not free of every trace of self-conceit.

One here must offer help wherever it is needed without display of one's support.

We neither wish to know the helper's name, nor hear of the assistance that was offered.

Within the Spirit's realm alone shall every helpful deed be duly judged, and only in the Spirit shall any helper's name be known.

GIVING THANKS

Once and a thousand times
Will the One Everlasting
Source inexhaustible,
Who gives without measure,
Give all of Himself:
And yet shall He always
Be wholly His own.

There is no dividing
What now and forever
Shall only be One.

Whenever He will
Make a gift of Himself
He gives Himself wholly.
How many times ever
He has given Himself,
Each time His gift
Was all of His Being.
And yet He remains

Forever His own,
Possessed by no other.
For not only once
Does the One Everlasting,
Source inexhaustible
Of gifts without measure,
Own his own Being.
Infinite Being Himself,
He likewise possesses
All of Himself
Infinite times.

As He is eternally
One in Himself:
In forms seeming infinite,
In essence but One,
So, too, in His light
We, Luminaries,
Are unified all:
A body whose members are many,
Whose life in the Spirit is One.

You: Boundless Source of Blessings,
Fountain of Light,
Light of Eternity,
You only judge one "sin":
Not to desire the treasures You grant
And want to bestow without ceasing.

Giving Thanks

You want no more than
Open hands,
Receptive, willing hearts;
Hands that accept with joy,
Hearts receiving Your bounty
With gladness.

You give to one,
And give to another
Wealth without measure;
And none shall be wanting
What others receive.

Whoever has known You,
Source of all blessings,
Can harbor no envy.
Far more than anyone
Has strength to carry
You give of Your treasures,
And nothing can ever
Diminish Your wealth.

Those You love most
Who always desire
More of Your gifts.
On them You bestow
Even Yourself.

For You possess wealth
To give treasures to all;
And never shall You be the poorer
For those who desire Your gifts.

You: Light Everlasting,
Infinite Fountain of Gifts.

༄

EPILOGUE

Nine years ago *The Book on the Living God* was published in its first edition.* It has since then gained many friends throughout the world who gratefully received the guidance it provides.

The present work is a revised edition, based on a newly written and expanded manuscript.†

The contents of the first edition have remained unchanged.

But many things are now presented in a different way, because it gradually became apparent that one word or another of the former text allowed a reading that was manifestly not intended.

**Das Buch vom lebendigen Gott*, München: Kurt Wolff, Verlag der Weissen Bücher, 1919.

†*Das Buch vom lebendigen Gott*, Basel-Leipzig: Kober'sche Verlagsbuchhandlung, 1927.

Time also proved that other parts had been presented too concisely, so that it seemed appropriate to expand on certain topics; finally, each word has once again been carefully examined, to ensure its meaning cannot be misread.

Furthermore, the inner harmony of the entire work demanded changes in the sequence of its chapters, together with an ordering of the text whereby essential points are shown more clearly to the reader's eye; given that in all my writings I am spiritually *speaking* to the reader and, consequently, must employ devices of typography* that may awaken the experience of hearing the text as if it is being spoken within.

I am grateful to all readers who had shown me what still needed explanation; for a sentence doubtless will read differently if one already is familiar with its intended meaning from actual experience, or if its substance has to be intuitively fathomed by a soul still lacking that experience.

Readers, on the other hand, who feel they must exert their subtlety of mind to make out contra-

---

*For example, Bô Yin Râ often used dashes at the end of sentences to indicate that the "speaker" is pausing before going on to the next sentence. Such typographical devices have not been carried over to the English translation.

Epilogue

dictions in my words would do better to allow that even I might well have noticed what they consider such remarkable discoveries.

More profitable would it be for them to reconcile, by their own lights, what they believe are "contradictions," recognizing that I must have had good reasons if at times I let a passage stand from which it would be easy to construe apparent contradictions as long as one has not yet grasped what at this point one ought to have already understood.

༄

I HERE WOULD also clearly stress that this enlarged edition is henceforth meant to supersede the former version of this book; indeed, in its expanded form, one might compare it to its first edition the way that a cathedral, completely finished in all parts, compares to its unfinished state, when it is still without its stained glass windows, and lacking statues on its altars.

And so *The Book on the Living God*, in its perfected form and new appearance, will doubtless bring enrichment even to all those who long have known it in its former shape.

That it truly is a book of which the world today has dire need is gratefully affirmed by countless readers who found strength and comfort in its pages.

Blessings, light, and inner certainty shall it impart to all who are resolved to read and to receive it without prejudice.

Late autumn 1927
BÔ YIN RÂ

REMINDER

"Yet here I must point out again that if one would derive the fullest benefit from studying the books I wrote to show the way into the Spirit, one has to read them in the original; even if this should require learning German.

"Translations can at best provide assistance in helping readers gradually perceive, even through the spirit of a different language, what I convey with the resources of my mother tongue."

From "Answers to Everyone" (1933), *Gleanings*. Bern: Kober'sche Verlagsbuchhandlung, 1990

EDITORS' NOTE TO THE SECOND EDITION

As was customary in his day, Bô Yin Râ referred to the male gender in his books when addressing both men and women. When speaking of individuals, for example, he uses "he" and "him" although his message is intended for both genders. But Bô Yin Râ's writings make it absolutely clear that the inner path he describes—the path that leads to the birth of the Living God within— is equally open to men and women. He is unequivocal in condemning the notion of male superiority and the oppression of women by men. He also makes it clear that God is not an anthropomorphic, gendered being but, rather, the source of all being, encompassing both male and female polarities.

In this second edition of the original English translation, we have used a gender-neutral approach. Our intention was twofold: to bring Bô Yin Râ's writing into harmony with current consciousness and practice, and to realize his intended meaning.

There are, however, three instances in which the masculine pronoun has been retained. When quoting from the King James Version of the

Bible, or other sources in which the masculine pronoun is used, we have, of course, not altered the original. We have also retained the masculine pronoun in Bô Yin Râ's poem, "Giving Thanks," in order to maintain its literary integrity. Finally, we continue to use the masculine pronoun when referring to the Luminaries, or inner guides. Bô Yin Râ explains that, here on earth, a Luminary requires a male body in order to function. As a spiritual entity, however, the Luminary consists of female and male poles united. A more complete explanation of these concepts can be found in *The Book On Human Nature*.

M.W. and E.W.S., Editors

The Book on Human Nature,
The Book on Life Beyond and this book
form a trilogy.

These three books should be
read together.

A description of
The Book on Human Nature and
The Book On Life Beyond follows.

The Book on Human Nature

The Book on Human Nature presents basic concepts about human nature with the goal of inspiring readers to awaken the timeless, spiritual spark within. We become fully human only when the spiritual potential within us gradually awakens and infuses our material, purely animal selves. It is a path that every human being may and should pursue.

A central understanding is that all life results from the joining of opposites, in particular, the polarity of male and female energies. Bô Yin Râ emphasizes that the true spiritual human being is male and female united in one entity; when we seek our spiritual self, we must call forth the male and female in ourselves and in all things. He discusses the biblical fall from grace as a descent from the spiritual plane, in which male and female were united, onto a material plane, in which male and female are split apart.

Bô Yin Râ warns men that holding onto the illusion of male superiority means forfeiting their spiritual life. While the spiritual paths that are natural for men and women are different in tone—open and receptive for women, active and grasping for men—they are equal and complementary. He tells us that *true* marriage is preparation for the life beyond: by coordinating the desires, wills and attitudes of two beings we once again bring about, in some measure, the original state in which male and female energies are united.

E.W.S. Publisher

Contents: Introduction. The Mystery Enshrouding Male and Female. The Path of the Female. The Path of the Male. Marriage. Children. The Human Being of the Age to Come. Epilogue. A Final Word.

The Book on Life Beyond

The Book on Life Beyond is a guide to help readers understand what they can expect to find in the life beyond death, and how to best prepare for it.

Bô Yin Râ explains that life beyond is actually another dimension of the same life we know here on earth—just as real and solid, but perceived through spiritual, rather than our limited, physical senses. He emphasizes the direct connection between our actions here on earth and their effects on life beyond. We bring with us into life beyond the same state of inner being with which we departed, and are able to experience its wonders exactly to the degree to which we have developed our spiritual self. For example, those who have failed to show compassion for others and have lived selfishly will find that life beyond lacks the warmth and light that other, more developed souls can perceive.

Bô Yin Râ counsels us to mentally practice the "art of dying" as a meditative practice to prepare for the transition from physical to spiritual existence. The goal is to constantly orient one's thinking, emotions and desires toward transformation of the self, in order to be able to receive the spiritual help that will be available to us after death.

E.W.S. Publisher

Contents: Introduction. The Art of Dying. The Temple of Eternity and the World of Spirit. The Only Absolute Reality. What Should One Do?

THE KOBER
PRESS

CPSIA information can be obtained
at www.ICGtesting.com
Printed in the USA
LVHW110942040821
694515LV00004B/12/J